Real Estate Street Smarts

Is brought to you by

Kennen Pyne & Jeff Bates

Real Estate Consumer Advocates
at Stonebrook Real Estate
Real Estate Licensees for the State of Utah
Founders of RESmartMoves.com

But more importantly...

Son
Brother
Husband
Father
Friend

...because the focus of this book is to help those we care about do well in real estate. We hope this information will help you and those you care about.

-DISCLAIMER-

Every effort has been made to ensure data is accurate and relevant in this book. It has been written with our family, friends, and consumers in mind. Realize laws change, circumstances vary, and there is always a chance for error. This book should not be taken as a consultation for your specific situation. Real estate transactions have many factors that affect their outcome and this book does not contain all the answers you will need. It is a great resource to increase your knowledge, but should not replace consulting with the proper professionals.

Using the information in this book along with competent professionals will give you an advantage. You will feel confident in your next real estate move. No one can predict the future, but arming yourself with knowledge and finding the best professionals to work with, when you need one, will help you make Smart Moves in real estate!

Realtor ® is a trademark of the National Association of Realtors ® (NAR), and anyone using that term as a part of his professional identity must be a member, not only of the NAR, but his local and state associations.

Mortgage-X and Mortgage-x.com are property of their respective owners. Specific content herein has been used with permission following their publishing guidelines. RESmartMoves.com encourages you to visit Mortgage-X site at www.mortgage-x.com as we do with all the webites referenced in our book and on our website, www.RESmartMoves.com.

RESmartMoves.com is owned and operated by Jeff Bates and Kennen Pyne, Realtors licensed in the state of Utah.

Real Estate Street Smarts

Introduction

The purpose of this book is to provide you with knowledge and Real Estate Street Smarts so you will know when to make a move and when not to, and when you do move, to make sure you do not fall victim to the many pitfalls that surround you. This book will prepare you to make smart moves in real estate that will meet your housing needs and build your own personal wealth and security.

There are so many factors to consider in real estate when you are planning for current and future housing needs. It is not always better to buy real estate. Sometimes you are better off renting. You will learn how to determine this for yourself. This skill alone will save you more money and stress than you can imagine.

From our work as consultants, salespeople, and as consumers we know how great and how terrible real estate can be for individuals and families. It can lift as well as destroy finances, not to mention peace of mind. Some mishaps are minor, but some are major. You can lose everything you have as a result of one real estate transaction.

 Before I became a licensed Realtor I experienced a little of the painful side of real estate. I remember being upset at the closing of our first home. I was a young, inexperienced consumer. It was our first home loan. I did not know what normal and acceptable loan terms were. I did not have the smarts to have someone that was more experienced helping me. No Father, Mother, Realtor or Friend. They would have come if I had asked them to. It was just my young wife and I, the private seller, the title company, and our mortgage guy. At closing the lender sprung a .33% increased interest rate and a 15-year balloon payment clause. He also charged us 2.5% instead of the normal 1% origination fee. We did not know what normal was. I am sure he saw us coming. We also did not know lenders make money on the back end of the loan as well. They call it a yield spread and I bet he also did very well on that. I was upset but did not know I could hold up the show to get him to fix it. This was not a major event but it left a mark.

This was the first part of our education and many other lessons followed. A few home purchases and years later I became a licensed Agent and Realtor. Many more opportunities followed to learn from personal experience and watching others experience the good, bad, and the down right ugly!

As a consumer you need to understand what motivates the people you work with and understand how they are rewarded. Your knowledge of the real estate industry will go a long way to help you stay out of trouble. When you realize how the system works and learn the tricks of the trade, you will recognize good, honest, and skilled professionals. You will be able to detect those who are willing to throw you under a bus to get what they want. There are so many good people to work with- there is no need to work with professionals that would harm you for their gain.

The best person to look out for you is **you!** You will learn how to trust but verify the information you are given before you make a decision. We believe many things that are not completely true and some that are completely wrong.

If you do not know what to ask and look for you become an easy target for those who would take advantage of you. Whether on purpose or accident it does not matter, because the end result is the same. It is your family that suffers, not theirs. There are many professionals, real estate agents, lenders, appraisers, title companies and others that get in trouble. When and if they are caught they may be disciplined, lose their license, get fined, and possibly go to jail. They are a small percentage of the professionals available to help you. Most professionals are good and some are great.

Working with great people will make a huge difference. This book will help you know how to find great people and help you know what to look for. Your personal knowledge of the process and workings of the industry will pay off big time, because even the best and the most honest salespeople are motivated by their own needs and interests. Sales training in many, if not all industries is to help salespeople motivate customers to buy. They are salespeople, is it even their place to tell you when you shouldn't buy? I will let you answer that question.

It will always be a good time to buy or sell to a salesperson. You need to know how to evaluate your options and determine if buying, selling or renting is the best choice for you. You will know when to buy or sell, and when it is the right time, you will get the right type of property at the right terms and price.

Real estate, for most people is the largest transaction they will ever make. The knowledge you have will help you make wise choices and keep you out of risky or destructive situations. The chapter on loan fraud will help keep you from paying fines, or even jail time, for an innocent mistake that the Federal Government does not like. Ignorance is not bliss. Loan fraud is a federal crime.

No one wants to get ripped off. There are many scams out there. These scam artists are very creative, they are always thinking of new ways to steal from you. You don't want to be the guy that bought a piece of land only to find out the owner sold it four times to four separate people. Your money is gone and the land ownership is in question. You will learn how to avoid these potential disasters.

Real estate can and should be a great part of your enjoyment of life, in building wealth, and security for your family. As an educated consumer you will make better buying and selling choices. This will save you thousands of dollars and a lot of headaches. It can also save you from a total disaster. If you ask around I know you will hear some horror stories. Sure there will be small bumps in the road as you learn from real life experiences, the key is to avoid the large bumps and the cliffs that are out there. It is a lot like mountain biking. You will do well to avoid the large rocks and trees and not worry about the small rocks and branches on the trail. If you focus too much on the small stuff you end up running into a large rock or end up in the trees. This may sound a little scary but it is very fun! Real estate can also be a lot of fun, and will prove to be the best investment you can make for your future success and well being.

We don't want you to have any horror stories to tell. Lets leave those stories to the people who don't like to read. Thank you for reading this book. We hope the information will help you as much as it has helped us.

This book is not meant to take the place of help from the proper professionals. It is meant, as a general base of knowledge that will help you know which questions to ask to get the information you need for your specific situation. There are so many factors that make transactions different. You are advised to consult with local professionals when you evaluate your situation and options.

Whether you decide to hire someone to help you or if you do it yourself you will benefit from all you learn. If you have any suggestions or comments please send them to **StreetSmarts@RESmartMoves.com**

REAL ESTATE STREET SMARTS

~ CONTENTS ~

Real Estate Street Smarts

-Chapter 1-
WHEN IT IS SMART TO RENT, AND WHEN YOU SHOULD BUY

There are pros and cons for both renting and buying a home. There is a good reason why more people in the United States own homes instead of renting them. We will first consider why it is so great to own real estate and we will also explain when it is smarter to rent. And we really mean SMART to rent real estate. At the end of this chapter you will know how to calculate for yourself which choice is best for you. The answer will change as your life changes. You can plan this change and truly build your own personal wealth and freedom.

Why buy? Buying a home provides shelter for your family and works for you, as an investment. For most people it is the largest source of wealth they have, however it is not always best to buy a home. There are times when you are better off financially to rent instead. More on that later in this chapter.

Strange enough, it is fact that real estate provides shelter that makes your home a great investment. As the population grows, children grow up and move into their own place, so the demand for housing increases. It is one of the basic needs we all have along with food and clothing.

Owning your home offers you some important lifestyle advantages over renting. When you rent a home the landlord makes the rules for you to follow with regard to the home. In most cases you can't customize the home to fit your needs, nor would you want to spend the money or time on the improvements.

When you own, you are in control. If you want to put up or take down a fence you can do it. You can even have a pet! The only people you have to answer to is the City or County you are in if they have restrictions, and the Home Owners Association (HOA) if you have one. You can decorate, modify, and improve the property to your specific needs.

Owning your home gives you control of your housing. When you rent a home the rental or lease agreement is for a period of time, usually a year or two. They can also be month to month. In all cases you only have the right to live there for the term of the contract. After the term of the contract the landlord (owner) can give you a notice to move.

The landlord can also increase your rent at the end of your contract. History shows just as the cost to buy real estate has gone up so has the cost to rent. The use and control of the property is wonderful, not to mention the pride you feel when you own a piece of this beautiful earth! When you realize what else real estate can do for you, you will be amazed.

Think about it financially. The cost to buy real estate goes up and down like any investment market. It spends more time going up than it does going down because of the strong demand. Long-term real estate investments average five percent increases per year. This average includes years that increase at twenty percent, some at two percent, some that it actually drops ten percent or more in a year, but over the long term it increases.

For example, if you are 30 years old when you buy your home you can expect the prices to double twice before you turn 60. Your monthly cost and total cost can and should be fixed. Most people get a loan to buy their home. The typical loan is for thirty years. At the end of the thirty years you no longer have a loan payment, you only have taxes, property insurance, and HOA fees if applicable. Your income level likely will increase as you age, and your housing costs stay basically the same until that great day when your home is paid off and you own it free and clear. The best home you can own is one that is paid for.

You can test the reality of appreciation very easily by asking people you know and trust how much they paid for their home and what year they bought it. You should also ask how much they paid in monthly rent before they purchased a home. After you do this a few times you will be able to see what we are talking about.

When I was discovering real estate for myself I learned that my grandparents paid six thousand dollars for their small brick home in the 1940's. In the late 90's the home sold for one hundred thousand. In a fifty year period this home doubled in price four times. The street I grew up on has homes that were built new in the late sixties and early seventies in the low to mid twenty thousand-dollar range. In the latest cycle at the peak similar homes sold for over two hundred and twenty thousand dollars and have since dropped to the two hundred thousand dollar range. In forty years these homes doubled in price three times. Are you starting to see a trend?

Average Sold Price Per Square Foot in Utah County, Utah

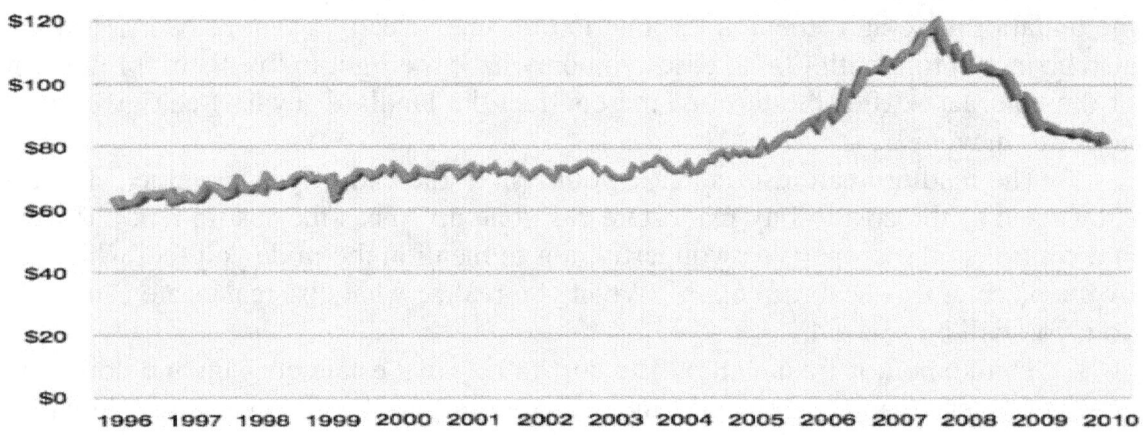

Real Estate Street Smarts

When I first started selling homes as a Realtor I asked a seasoned agent at the office if he would mind if I had a look at his old listing books. I only had statistics up to 1995 available on the Internet system we now use, so with these old books that contained sold and active listings I was able to look back in time in my local area and see the reality of increased cost at this rate that I have described. It was important to me to know that what I was selling was good and that it would help people make better lives for themselves.

When you have a home that is paid off, and is worth four times or more than what you paid for it, you have built significant wealth. What financial freedom it gives you in your life to have a fixed payment that feels expensive at first but soon becomes inexpensive as rents and purchase prices go up.

If you do not buy a home and always rent you will not have the risk of a mortgage but you will have the high risk of raised rent. If you rent for thirty years your rent will also double twice. You will have paid for a home in the amount of rent over the years but will have nothing to show for it. If you do not believe this ask around, and you can learn this for yourself.

You can blame it on inflation if you want to, but rather than that I recommend that you embrace inflation and let it work its magic for you. Like many worthwhile things it can be painful at first. At first buying is more expensive than renting. After ten years it is less expensive because your cost is fixed and prices have likely gone up. Twenty years later you are the envy of all homebuyers wishing they had purchased 20 years ago when prices were so good. And the amazing feeling of real wealth is when you look at the current prices of renting and buying and say to yourself "I don't know how people do it"? Your house is paid off and your money goes toward retirement investments and having more fun than you deserve.

There are ups and downs. Real estate is a long-term investment. In a sellers market you have to own the home for 1-3 years to break even because of the costs to buy and sell. In a buyers market, where the supply is high and demand is low, it could take many more years to break even. You can lose incredible amounts of money if your timing is bad.

There are places in the United States that do not have population and demand increases. These areas do not offer the increased prices, but they still offer the wealth of no mortgage when the home is paid off.

Owning is a great way to minimize the cost of housing over your lifetime. It can also be a great investment and part of your retirement plan. Take a look at the upside for the landlord. The renter makes rent payments that pay a portion, all, or more than the mortgage on the property. In thirty years or less it is paid for and as rent increases there is more income for the owner. Yes there is a down side also.

7

Real Estate Street Smarts

The landlord is responsible for the property, financially, and for its care. There is risk involved with any investment; physical damage and financial loss are possible for any landlord.

When you own your property you are the boss. You decide when to move. Real estate investments are best when they are long term. The risk is, in my opinion, too high when you are not planning on keeping the property for 3 or more years. Ten years is best. But the incredible returns come after that.

Is there anything better than planting a garden if you want one? Maybe you want to put in a basketball pad, a hot tub, gazebo, grass, fruit trees or whatever. Your home serves your family as a place of memories, a place of comfort, security, stability, and protection. There are very few things that are needed more than a home!

You must evaluate the cost of housing and your own personal situation to know what will be best for you. To buy you must be prepared, in the right situation personally, and have the costs and risks of owning the home make sense.

Renting a home is the right choice sometimes. Timing is the key and RISK is the reason. Homes go up and down in value as the supply and demand change. In a real estate market that has experienced either significant increases in the supply of homes or a significant decrease in demand (buyers), or both, home prices decline. There are many reasons for this; we will go into detail in chapter two. The key here is understanding that prices can fall quickly. It is a normal part of the cycle. It is usually short lived with most years increasing in value or staying the same, but if you buy and sell at the wrong time you can lose a lot of money.

It is not abnormal in this type of market to have a ten to twenty percent decrease in one year. That would be twenty to forty thousand dollars in one year on a two hundred thousand dollar home. It is most rewarding to rent when prices are falling and you do not already own a home.

Before you decide to buy or rent, you must ask yourself some questions and do some planning. You may not know all the answers and that is okay. Start by evaluating the market statistics in your area to determine if you are in an increasing, stable, or a decreasing market. This can change but after you read chapter two you will have a good understanding of where you are in the cycle.

The next thing to consider is how long you expect to keep the home. Notice we did not say live in the home. Owning the home and living in the home are two different things as long as you are okay with being responsible for the home as a landlord. The longer you own the home the less risky the investment becomes.

It really is a matter of simple math. If you are living in an area for a short

Real Estate Street Smarts

term of one to three years buying a home is very risky. Take a look at the cost. To rent a home you will need a deposit that is typically close to the amount of one months rent, you will need the first months rent, and you may need last months rent up front. For a home that rents for $1,200 a month this is an estimated cost of $3,425.

In declining markets landlords may also be motivated to get renters in to cover their costs. They may offer incentives like first months rent free, a signing bonus or a discounted monthly rent amount to fill the vacancy.

Your cost monthly is twelve hundred dollars for rent. When you move three years later, at the end of your lease, the landlord will check the condition of the home and will give you your deposit minus the damage that needs to be repaired for the next renters. Having carpets that need to be cleaned is very typical. Even if the landlord kept your entire deposit, and they usually don't, your cost for the place would be twelve hundred a month plus approximately one thousand dollars.

Look how much you would have spent buying a home in this same period. First you have a down payment of 3.5 to 5 percent. You also have closing cost with the title company and the lender. For this example we will assume the buyer negotiates to have the three percent for closing cost paid for by the seller of the home they buy. We will also assume the home is listed and there is no cost to the buyer to have a buyers agent help them.

A similar home is likely to be $200,000 so the down payment would be at least 7,000. With low interest rates, if you are fortunate to have low rates at the time, you are looking at $1200 a month for a loan of $200,000 at 6 percent. If the rates are at 12 % your cost doubles but rents would also increase. For this example we will use 6%. You also have property taxes, mortgage insurance, and property insurance that will add approximately $150 monthly for this type of home. Some homes also belong to an HOA (Home Owners Association) and have fees that go to the HOA to cover common area amenities and services.

When you decide to sell the home you have title insurance and recording fees to pay that will cost about 1 % of the sales price and if you hire a real estate agent to sell the home they charge around 6% of the purchase price.

Your cost to have the property month to month is about the same. Renting is a little less. The big difference is the cost to buy and sell the home. $9,000 to $20,000 estimated cost to buy and sell depending on if you do it yourself or hire a professional. Either way you are looking at one thousand, some of which you may get back, versus nine to twenty thousand to buy.

Real Estate Street Smarts

Upfront Cost To Rent A Basic Home

$ 1,200	Monthly rent
$ 1,000	Deposit (you may get most of this back)
$ 25	Application fee (some landlords may charge)
$ 1,200	Last months rent (some may require)
$ -	Cost to break lease (if applicable, depending on situation)

$ 3,425 Total upfront cost

Upfront Cost To Buy A Similar Home ($200,000)

$ 7,000	Down payment, 3.5% or more
$ -	Closing costs to get loan etc. seller may pay for you
$ 600	Inspection and other cost to evaluate purchase
$ -	Commission to buyers agent, usually no cost

$ 7,600 Total out of pocket cost best case scenario
(cost to sell at later date not included)

$ 7,600	Total estimated best case scenario cost
$ 6,000	Closing costs to get loan etc. 3%
$ 6,000	Commission to buyers agent 3%

$19,600 Total out of pocket cost worst case scenario
(cost to sell at later date not included)

That is only part of the equation. When you own the home you have the risk and reward of price changes. If prices went up at 20% in three years you would actually make money when you sold your home. At a 10% increase in value you almost broke even. If the prices stayed the same you lost 10% and if they dropped 20% you would lose a crazy total of 30% with the costs to buy, sell, and the price change factored in. That is $60,000. If it only lost 10% you are still looking at losing $40,000. If prices stayed the same you would lose $20,000.

Real Estate Street Smarts

Total Cost To Rent for 3 Years, Annual Lease

$	42,000	Monthly rent for 3 years, excludes last month
$	1,000	Deposit, you may get some of this back
$	1,200	Last months rent
$	25	Application fee
$	7,200	Cost to terminate lease early, this should be high
$	250	Repairs, this cost will depend on your lease terms
$	**51,675**	**Total cost for 3 years**
$	(7,200)	No charge for breaking lease
$	**44,475**	**Expected Total cost for 3 years**
	1,231	Total cost stated monthly.

($ in parentheses) *Are a credit to your cost, not charged, or money you get back.*

Total cost to own for 3 years

$	7,000	Down payment, 3.5% or more
$	6,000	Closing costs to get loan etc. 3%
$	2,000	Closing cost to sell home 1%, title fees, insurance etc.
$	12,000	Cost to hire a professional to sell your home 6% (this can vary)
$	48,600	Mortgage payment (1,350) including taxes and insurance for 3 years
$	(3,600)	Estimated tax savings currently offered for the interest portion of your loan
$	(7,600)	Amount paid down on your mortgage loan
$	(7,000)	Down payment you get back when you sell
$	**57,400**	**Expected total cost in flat market, no home price increase or loss.**
	1,594	Total cost stated monthly.
$	57,400	Flat market cost
$	40,000	Cost increase from 20% decline in home sales price
$	**97,400**	**Total cost after the 20% loss of home value.**
	2,705	Total cost stated monthly.
$	57,400	Flat market cost
$	-40,000	Cost decrease from 20% increase in home sales price
$	**17,400**	**Total cost after 20% increase in home value** .
	483	Total cost stated monthly.

You can see from the numbers that the smart person is the renter, risking only $1,000 dollars on the deposit with his, hopefully kind, landlord. How long you need to keep the home for you to make money will depend on the part of the cycle you are in and the actual market activity. Markets can change at any time.

Real Estate Street Smarts

The reality is that short-term ownership of a few years is very risky. It takes time to break even on your costs. In a great market you can break even on these costs and start to make money in less than a year, but are you willing to risk it? Safe investments will work steadily to build wealth for you. Risky investments have a tendency to destroy finances.

Rental Cost for 15 Years

$	216,000	Monthly rent for 15 years with no rent increases!
$	1,000	Deposit
$	25	Application fee
$	-	Cost to break lease
$	1,250	Repairs, this will depend on the lease terms
$	**218,275**	**Total effective cost for housing with no rent increase**
	1,212	Total effective monthly cost for housing with no rent increases.

Ownership cost for 15 years

$	7,000	Down payment, 3.5% or more
$	6,000	Closing costs to get loan etc. 3%
$	4,000	Closing cost to sell home 1%, title fees, insurance etc.
$	24,000	Cost to hire a professional to sell your home 6% (this can vary)
$	243,000	Mortgage payment (1,350) including taxes and insurance for 15 years
$	(18,000)	Estimated tax savings currently offered for the interest portion of your loan
$	(56,000)	Amount paid down on your mortgage loan
$	(200,000)	Estimated value of the home will have doubled, 400 k
$	(7,000)	Down payment money you get back when you sell
$	9,000	Total repair cost at 50 dollars per month for 15 years
$	**12,000**	**Total effective cost for housing for 15 years**
	67	Total effective monthly cost for 15 years after cashing out, selling your home.

Rental Cost For 30 Years

$	432,000	Monthly rent for 30 years with no rent increases!
$	1,000	Deposit
$	25	Application fee
$	-	Cost to break lease
$	10,000	Repairs, this will depend on the lease terms
$	**443,025**	**Total effective cost for housing with no rent increase**
	1,231	Total effective monthly cost with no rent increases.

Real Estate Street Smarts

Ownership cost for 30 years

$ 7,000	Down payment, 3.5% or more
$ 6,000	Closing costs to get loan etc. 3%
$ 8,000	Closing cost to sell home 1%, title fees, insurance etc.
$ 48,000	Cost to hire a professional to sell your home 6% (this can vary)
$ 486,000	Mortgage payment (1,350) including taxes and insurance for 30 years
$ (36,000)	Estimated tax savings currently offered for the interest portion of your loan
$(200,000)	Amount paid down on your mortgage loan
$(600,000)	Estimated value increase (the home will have doubled twice, 800 k)
$ (7,000)	Down payment money you get back when you sell
$ 18,000	Total repair cost at 50 dollars per month for 30 years

(*$ in parentheses*) *Amounts you receive or benefit you and are not a cost to you.*

$(270,000)	**Total effective cost for housing for 30 years and now no mortgage payment!**
(*750*)	Total effective cost for 30 years after cashing out, selling your home, stated month

$270,000 in the black   **($270,000 in the positive!!)**

$713,025 **Effective Difference Between Renting And Owning 30 Years**

Because real estate cycles are usually seven to ten years long you stand to make money by owning the home if you plan to keep the home for five to ten years.

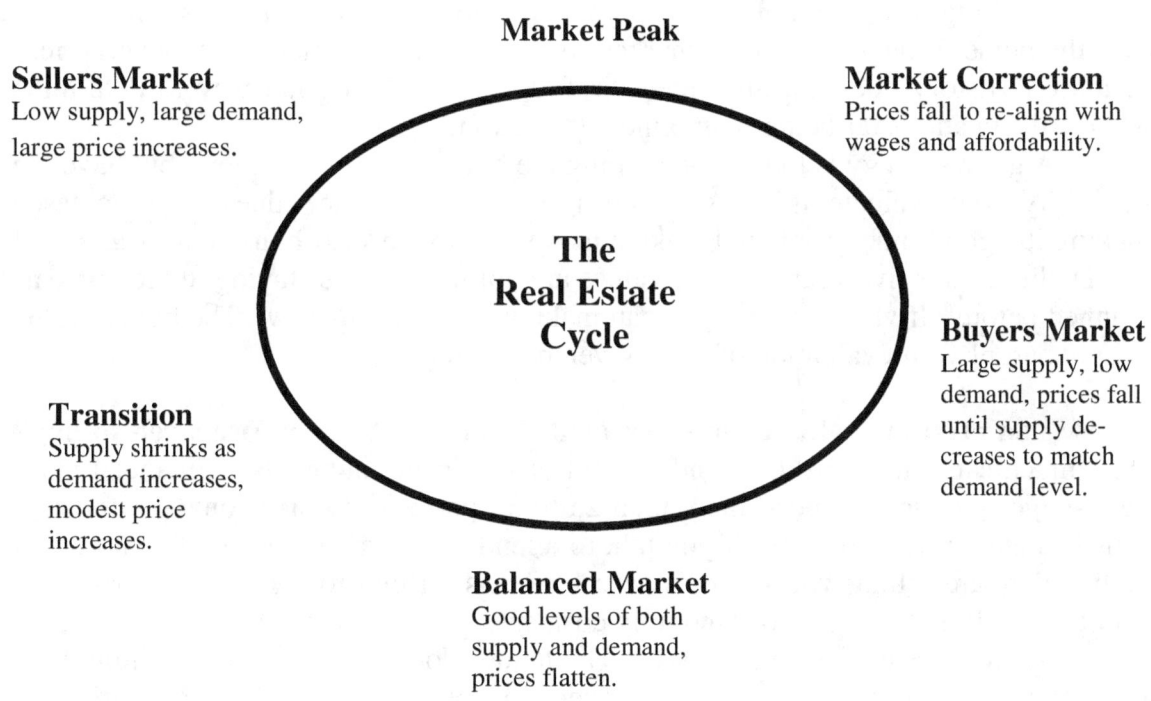

Market Peak

Sellers Market
Low supply, large demand, large price increases.

Market Correction
Prices fall to re-align with wages and affordability.

The Real Estate Cycle

Buyers Market
Large supply, low demand, prices fall until supply decreases to match demand level.

Transition
Supply shrinks as demand increases, modest price increases.

Balanced Market
Good levels of both supply and demand, prices flatten.

Longer is better. The longer you own the home the less risk of the value going below your purchase price.

Another thing to think about when you evaluate your choice to buy or rent is the fact that the owner is responsible, unless stated otherwise in a lease agreement, for the repairs of the property. Homes need care to keep their condition up. Roofs need to be repaired and some-times replaced. The weather out-side gradually takes it toll. Most

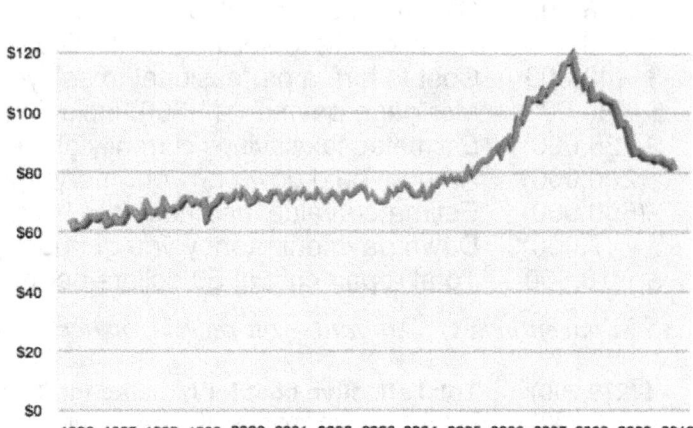

Average Sold Price Per Square Foot in Utah County, Utah

products have a life expectancy. Stucco is expected to be replaced after about 25 years. Furnaces usually last for 15 to 30 years and water heaters usually last 5 to 10 years. If you keep the home long enough these repairs are not a big deal. If the home is a short term investment and you have to repair the home it adds to your risk of fi-nancial loss.

Planning to own a home for 10 years or more is best as it gives you time to own the home through the sellers market portion of the real estate cycle when prices increase. History does not guarantee the future but it is a good way to determine what is likely and is far better than blind speculation.

A good strategy is to plan on owning the home ten years or more, but have the flexibility to re-evaluate as you go. During this period if the values have increased making it a good time to sell and make a move up to your next house that is great. If you evaluate after five years and the values are not up, you are staying in the home as planned before. If values are up you can make your move up now. The homes value is only part of your evaluation of buying versus renting.

You need to evaluate your personal situation. Are you prepared to buy? How much can you afford to spend on rent or mortgage payments? Financial plan-ners suggest we do not spend more than 25 to 35 percent of our income on housing. This is a good rule of thumb. If you talk to a lender who approves you for more just realize they are telling you what risk the lender is willing to take, not the risk you should be willing to take. Your monthly costs need to be comfortable.

Are you ready for a rainy day? The lender does not care if it is raining they just want their money! How much money do you have saved? If you are self-employed it is wise to have 12 months living expenses in savings just in case financial challenges come, and they will come at some time in your life. If you are not self-employed and have what you feel is a secure job you will not need as much in savings. Having 6 months living expenses in savings is recommended. This amount needs to account for housing costs of your new place if you are planning to buy or rent something more expensive than your current costs.

This money will give you stability and happiness because you will know that if something bad happens you have time to take care of the problem and make corrections. To illustrate the importance of this just think of the average employee that experiences the loss of their employment. Your monthly bills still come, but the monthly wage is gone. Sure you can go find a new job, but this takes a little time and effort. If you have the money you need for six months of normal living expenses you can cut back on spending and work hard to replace or increase your income earnings.

You may have to take a pay cut. If this is the case you have your savings to help you get through while you make changes to your income or expenses. This savings account is insurance for your well being and your housing investment.

What would happen if you lost your income and could not make your house payment? The bank has a lien on your home securing the loan. If the loan is not paid they can take the house to get their money by selling it. You can lose everything and be forced to start over with bad credit. You are better off renting until you have your savings in place.

That is not all you need. Remember earlier we talked about down payment and closing costs. Loan programs can change but right now you need 3.5% to 5% down for your home. You may be able to get 100% financing with a rural loan, but you will need to check with a lender to find out what your options are. Closing cost are usually about 3% and can be paid for by the seller in some situations. These amounts must be above and separate from your personal savings for a rainy day. Buying a home without these savings is very risky and can put your family in a situation much worse than renting.

To grow wealth you must be a strong tree with a strong root system. When the storms come you will still be standing and growing. A large tree without a good root system will fall and it will make a huge mess for you and for those you care about. Having savings and living within a good budget will give you a strong root system.

Do you live on a budget? Your investment will only be as good as your ability to run your personal finances. Homes have been used for personal and family bail outs with home equity loans and second mortgages. If you cannot live within your sensible budget you risk your home. This is a crucial part of your root system. It provides peace of mind, security, and wealth.

There are many great resources online, in bookstores, and on the radio that will help you understand sound principles for finances and budgeting. Learn and live the principles of healthy finances.

There is a time and a place for everything. Wealthy people have rented during their life time. It is a great and wonderful thing when the time is right. The same is true for owning your home when the time is right. Don't rush, be patient, and build strong. By doing this you will get wealthy must faster. The story of the Tortoise and the Hare comes to mind. Just for fun you should ask around to see if you know anyone who has lived this life lesson already for themselves or knows someone who has. We can avoid many problems by learning from others. History is a wonderful educator.

If the time is not right for you to buy, start preparing because it will be soon. By building strong you will build wealth much faster and will be much happier in the process. You should buy a home when the time is right for you, not for any other reason. If we had a RISK-O-METER, that functioned much like a SPEED-O-METER, we could look at the risk we take with our own personal debt choices. When we are going to fast it would remind us to slow down. We will get their much faster and in one piece if we drive smart. Even a speeding ticket causes a delay in your arrival, not to mention the fact that some people don't make it to their destination at all!

You need to be a smart renter. You can have setbacks renting if done unwisely. At our website (**www.RESmartMoves.com**) you can download a free report called SMART MOVES SMART RENTERS. It is a must read before you find a rental and sign a contract! It will help you avoid common problems renters have and help you look out for your best interest, save money and live better. This will help you become a buyer sooner and will help you enjoy the home you rent. Don't forget to download your free report before you make your move.

Real Estate Street Smarts

-Chapter 2-
How The Real Estate Market Works

The real estate market is like other markets. It is driven by the supply and demand of the product. It is both simple and complicated. Simply put, market value is determined by what a buyer is willing to pay and a seller is willing to accept.

Competition is at the heart of any market. Sellers are all competing for buyers. If a seller picks a price that is well above other similar homes buyers will prefer other homes at better prices. Buyers are limited to what sellers are willing to take. When the buyer and the seller come to an agreement you have market value.

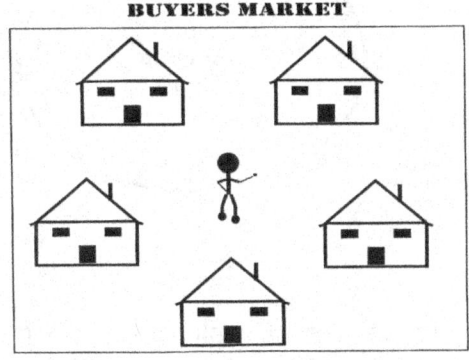

BUYERS MARKET

When the supply is large and demand is low it is called a buyers market. The advantage is to the buyer. The buyer has many homes to choose from, making it easier to find a home that matches their needs and lifestyle. In this market, prices are going down, staying about the same, or slowly increasing, depending on the exact market situation.

The sellers in a buyers market must be aggressive to entice a buyer to buy their home instead of another home. In these markets the homes tend to be better cleaned and prepared for the sale. In a buyers market you are more likely to be able to get the seller to pay the buyers closing costs. It is easier to get appliances included with the sale, and they may even have other incentives available. In a buyers market the <u>buyer</u> is in high demand.

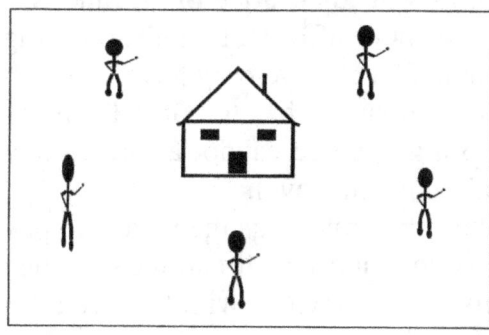

SELLERS MARKET

A sellers market is the opposite. The sellers have more control. The supply of homes is low and the demand is high. Buyers have to compete with many other buyers for the same homes. The seller can ask for more than the last home that sold and the buyer will pay more to be the one lucky buyer that actually gets the house. The selection is not as good in a sellers market. The great houses sell super fast and even average homes sell much faster than they would in a buyers market.

Buyers in their offers must try to be attractive to the sellers so they will pick them. Sellers list their homes a little higher than the sold homes they compare to.

Real Estate Street Smarts

The buyers, in an effort to win the bid, offer full price or even more than full price to get the house. This drives the prices up and sometimes very quickly.

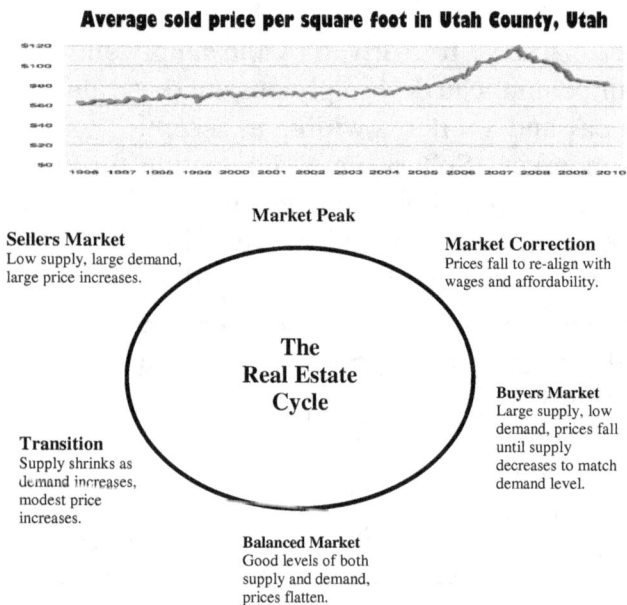

Average sold price per square foot in Utah County, Utah

Market Peak

Sellers Market
Low supply, large demand, large price increases.

Market Correction
Prices fall to re-align with wages and affordability.

The Real Estate Cycle

Buyers Market
Large supply, low demand, prices fall until supply decreases to match demand level.

Transition
Supply shrinks as demand increases, modest price increases.

Balanced Market
Good levels of both supply and demand, prices flatten.

This is the real estate cycle. It usually takes seven to ten years to get from the start to end of a cycle. The market is always changing. Sometimes slowly and sometimes very quickly. When it is a sellers market investors see the opportunity to buy or build homes. Developers come in and add to the inventory of homes (supply). The home price increase is very appealing, bringing more investors in. As the supply grows, the market will cool down from a hot sellers market to a buyers market again.

We all need a place to live. We have children and they need a place to live. People move in from out of town. Companies come in bringing jobs and people for those jobs. All these things increase the demand in the market. When the demand builds or supply shrinks the market changes again.

As prices change in a sellers market with high yearly increases, home's become less affordable for the wages of the area. When the supply increases and the market turns to a buyers market the prices fall to become affordable again for the wages. You can watch this as you look at the median price of a home for your area compared to the median household income. When the median price of a home is 5 times the amount of the median income homes are more affordable and appealing than when they are 6 times the amount. It is a simple fact that we only have so much money to spend each month. If housing takes more money it has to come from another part of our budget. When the prices get too high people cannot afford to buy and the market changes. Home prices should parallel income level.

Jobs have a huge impact on the market. Our jobs provide us the means to pay for all of these homes. If your area experiences serious job loss it can have a huge impact on the local housing market. In Detroit this is very obvious with the struggles the car industry is going through right now. Areas that have population decreases should not expect strong demand.

You have heard of ghost towns. If the need for the location changes there goes the demand and the value. The homes will sit empty and gradually fall apart because no one wants them.

Homes are where they are. It is possible to move them but it is very expensive. So they are only appealing to people who want to be in the area. It is not like a stock that can have the same value to different people in different locations of the world.

Have you ever wondered why an old house goes up in value over time while an old car, mobile home, motor home, couch, television, computer, and an airplane go down in value? It is the land! The house itself, (the brick, rock, wallboard, moldings, roof, heating system) actually go down in value each year. It is a small amount compared to the increased value of the land. Keep an eye on vacant land prices in your area. If they are going up, the cost to build a new home goes up with it and as a result other available homes go up as well.

It is all based on what a buyer will pay. How much more will a buyer pay for a new home instead of a 5 year old house? A ten year old house? A hundred year old house? This is why the average home itself only goes down $500 to 1000 a year in most cases. If land prices are dropping, home prices are dropping. If land prices are going up so will the house prices. Land is a very limited supply item. You can't make more of it. We have what we have. Back in history there have been times when they found new land. We are well past that now.

Many different things affect the supply and demand. Most people do not have cash to buy their home. That would be great and we should all get there, but most people don't start with cash. Home mortgage financing terms have a huge impact on affordability for buyers and the appeal of home prices. To demonstrate, look at this chart that shows the difference in monthly cost with the different interest rates.

Monthly Cost for $200,000 loan

Interest Rate	Principle and Interest payment
4%	$954.83
5%	$1,073.64
6%	$1,199.10
7%	$1,330.60
8%	$1,467.53
10%	$1,755.14
12%	$2,057.23
14%	$2,369.74
16%	$2,689.51

Look how much the same house will cost monthly as the rate changes!

Real Estate Street Smarts

National Average Contract Mortgage Rate from 1963 to 2009

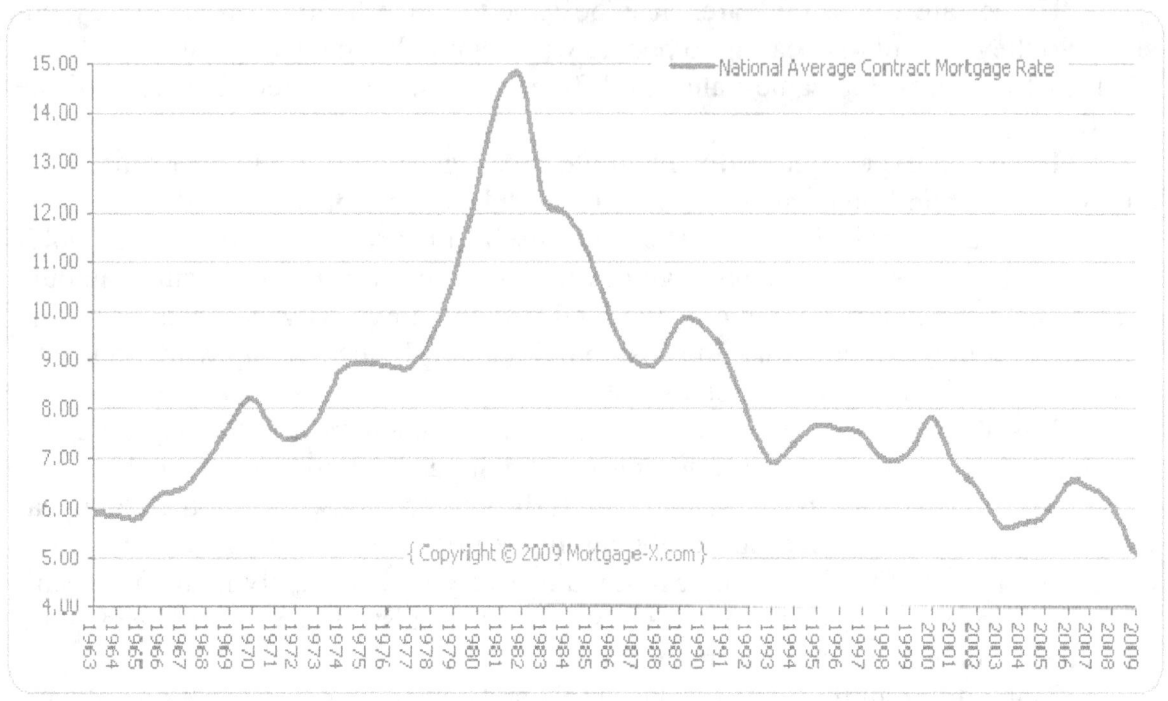

Courtesy of Mortgage-X.com

Notice what the interest rates have done in the past!

With a $1,200 monthly budget for principle and interest for your loan

Interest Rate	Loan amount with 1,200 payment
4%	$251,000
6%	$200,000
8%	$163,000
10%	$137,000
12%	$117,000
14%	$101,000
16%	$89,000

Look how much you get to spend on your house as rates change!

Local neighborhoods can be in a different part of the cycle because of unique demand and supply for the item. Homes can be very similar and they can be so incredibly unique and different.

Real Estate Street Smarts

     Before you buy you need to know what part of the cycle you are in and plan accordingly. Remember the ups and down are short term and true wealth is in your long term planning.

     Learning what to look for and how to work with real estate professionals will make a huge difference.

Real Estate Street Smarts

-Chapter 3-
The Inside Scoop On The Real Estate Industry.

Buying or selling a home can be a little overwhelming! It is helpful to know who is involved and what they do. Understanding their motivation and how they are paid for what they do will help you in your effort to look out for your own best interest.

It is important to mention that there are more good and honest professionals that care about you and your family doing well, than there are bad ones. The trick is to avoid those who would take advantage of you, throwing you under the bus, so to speak, for their own gain. Having a basic knowledge about the people who are helping you, and how their industry works will give you an advantage and truly help you avoid the few that would harm you.

You need to look out for yourself. No one cares about you and your family as much as you do. No one has the motivation for your success like you do and no one will be affected, as much as you are, by your progress as you make wise financial decisions and build wealth.

Everything we are told has a motive behind it. When you talk with professionals your understanding of who they are will give you a reference to help you value and weigh what they say. In our interaction with others we need to know what motivates them and how they are paid for what they do.

Mortgage Lenders: There are many people involved in real estate transactions. We will start with mortgage lenders. There are different types. Some lenders are called brokers. They don't work for a specific bank or credit union. They work for themselves and shop or broker out loan programs with the banks and institutions that lend the money. They usually have access to many loan programs and may have some programs they know well and like to use. Brokers also have lenders that work for them. The lenders who work for a broker pay a portion of what they make to the broker. lenders and brokers have processors who help submit all the information and paperwork needed to complete the loan.

There are lenders that work for credit unions and banks. They process loans that are offered by the company they work for. They have different market niches, construction loans, remodeling loans, purchase loans, refinance loans, bridge loans and more.

Some lenders co-broker loans, meaning they have another lender work the file until completion. They are paid a portion for bringing the borrower and completing their portion of the work.

With all lenders you should understand the fact that they make money on the front end by charging origination and processing fees and on the back end with what we call a yield spread. There is a difference in the interest rate the banks offer them and the rate they offer you. Interests rates fluctuate with supply and demand in the market. So when you get an estimate (called a good faith estimate) from a lender you can compare closing costs, interest rate, and loan program. If you get a quote at the same time from the lenders you are considering you can see what the differences are. If much time passes between the estimates the rates can change making your comparison like apples and oranges. Rates can even change through the course of a day.

Evaluate the numbers closely as the lender can make a lot of money off you by giving you a less appealing product. There are great lenders that are not trying to get rich off of you and are building their business on repeat customers. You will save a lot of money by avoiding lenders who would take advantage of you by charging large fees upfront and providing you with bad loan products.

There is nothing wrong with paying a good price for a good product. This is how capitalism works. It is how we all make a living. Competition is a great benefit of the system. You should know what programs and costs are available to you as a borrower. By checking the APR, Annual Percentage Rate, you can compare what the total cost of the money is for each loan. The APR calculates the interest you will pay plus any and all fees you will pay to secure the loan.

Normal cost for an origination fee is one percent of the loan amount. The total closing costs, if you are not buying down the interest rate (to lower your payments), should not be more than three percent for a conventional loan. FHA (Federal Housing Administration) loans are more because of the upfront mortgage insurance (1.5% of loan amount). If you do buy downs this increases your upfront cost. Buy downs are prepaid interest charges that drop your monthly payment for part or all of the loan repayment period. You can calculate how long you need to keep your loan to break even on your cost for the buy down. If you keep the loan longer than the break-even point it is a better deal.

Comparing the same loan programs is helpful. When comparing loan programs pay close attention to the APR on your good faith estimate. It will help you figure out which one is really the better deal.

Real Estate Street Smarts

When you have selected your lender and have a contract to purchase a home get a commitment from your lender in writing, lock in your rate/terms and make them stick to it. There are lenders who will raise the rate or ad fees at the closing table to make more money from you.

You can stop the closing and have them fix it. If you delay the closing you will need to consult with your advisers to see what implication you would have with the seller.

You have a deadline with the seller. You can lose the property or have increased cost and/or lost earnest money if you fail to close on the property within the terms of the contract. In some contracts the seller could also take legal action against you.

As with all professional services the reputation of the lender is important. Do they have a track record of doing what they say they will? Do they close on time without surprises at closing? Are they fair with their costs?

Title companies and Title insurance. When you buy a home the change in ownership is recorded on the county records in the county where the property is located. There are many laws that affect property and the title of property. In some states escrow companies and attorneys are used. In Utah Title companies handle the closing preparation, title search, title insurance, signed and notarized documents to be recorded, and follow contract instructions to comply with the terms of the contract to change ownership.

FOOD FOR THOUGHT

You receive better service when you are a good customer. By respecting professionals time and interests they will be motivated to take the same care of you and your family. What goes around comes around!

When you sign your closing papers the escrow officer can be an attorney but most are not. They are third parties that work to verify that the property can be sold. They follow the instructions given on the contract by both parties. They hold the money until the transaction is completed and disperse the funds to the appropriate places when it has been recorded. At the heart of what they do is the title search and insurance. The company has searchers who check the title of the property for anyone who would have an interest in it. They look for any liens on the property or anyone with ownership interest to the property. They notify both parties of the items recorded on the county records and give conditions and exemptions to their insurance policy on a preliminary report. The seller needs to have a clear title to sell the home to the new owner. The new owner does not want any liens that belong to the seller of the home. By law, workers who provide materials or labor for a home can file a mechanics lien if they are not paid in full. This is to help guarantee payment. By law, judgments against an individual can be attached to their home to ensure payment prior to selling or refinancing their home.

The title company provides an insurance policy. The costs vary based on the price of the home and the company providing the policy. This is a one-time fee paid at closing. For a $200,000 home the owners policy that covers the buyer is approximately $1,195, the lenders policy, paid by the buyer for the lender, is approximately $717. They also have an upgraded version that covers more items for an increased cost of 10%. Before you close you can go over the differences with the title company to make sure you buy the title insurance product you want.

Insurance is all about limiting your risk. You will have to decide if the cost of the upgraded policy is worth the reduction of risk. I would be careful buying a home without title work and insurance. It is not a good idea to risk it.

Title companies also charge fees for the work they do to facilitate the closing. The average cost for preparing the documents, the closing with a notary/escrow officer, mailing documents, wiring moneys, and recording with the county recorder is three hundred dollars. Prices can vary so you will want to check a few. You can ask a Realtor, or just call and ask title companies for a quote on an estimated sales price.

In every case you want to work with reputable companies that have a history of taking great care of their customers.

Realtors and Real Estate Agents/Brokers. Real Estate Agents are sales people who are licensed with their state to help people buy and sell homes located in their licensing state. To be licensed in the state of Utah you must be 18 or older, complete 90 hours of certified education and pass state required tests. agents must work under the supervision of a broker who has completed the state requirements for additional education (120 hours), met the minimum sales experience time period and number of closed transactions. They also must pass the state test for brokers.

A principal broker is the broker in charge of the agents at their office. An associate broker is a broker who is not in charge of the agents at their company but has met the requirements to be a broker. Agents and brokers must complete 18 hours of continuing education each time they renew their two-year license.

FOOD FOR THOUGHT

Do we ask professionals if they have any incentives available right now? This is a nice way to ask if they are flexible on their price?

Real Estate Street Smarts

A <u>Realtor</u> is an agent or broker that has joined the Association of Realtors. They are required to follow the higher standards regulated by the code of ethics put forth by the Association of Realtors. These rules and regulations go above and beyond the state regulations an agent must follow. They belong to a state association, national association, and to a local association and Multiple Listing Service you may know as an MLS.

Although the MLS is the most obvious difference it is only one difference. Realtors pay dues to help build their industry. They also give donations to help as the association lobbies with local, state and federal governments to protect the property rights of all Americans. It may be selfishly motivated, because if the government takes away your right to own your home we, as realtors, cannot get paid to sell it. Or it may be that we also see the wisdom and the power that comes from the rights we have as Americans to own property, to protect and provide for ourselves. It makes our country strong and provides opportunities for all of us.

FOOD FOR THOUGHT

In any industry the cost of products/services vary. Both the products/services and the price must be good to be a good value. One without the other will leave you with regrets.

Agents and Realtors who help buyers find a home to buy and coordinate all the details to help them throughout the process are called a <u>buyers agent</u>. They look out for the best interests of the buyer. It is not their job to look out for the seller. Services vary but can include helping a buyer get to know different areas, explain options they have, the pros and cons of different homes, viewing, selecting, negotiating, evaluating the property in the inspection period, coordinating the closing details, and help find solutions to problems that come up.

A <u>Listing Agent</u> looks out for the seller and helps them sell their home from start to finish. They do everything from helping price the property, preparing the property for showings, coordinating showings, providing feedback, advertising the home, negotiating contracts and more.

An agent that represents both the buyer and the seller... (I know what you are thinking. He said represents both. How do you do that?) It is called a limited agent or dual agent. The agent is limited to the things he can tell either party as it could weaken their negotiating positions. An attorney representing both sides would not fly in the courtroom, that is for sure.

The costs for these services vary widely. There are many different business models that include full service to partial service. We will go into great detail on this in the following chapters. The cost ranges from no cost to 10% of the price of the property. I think you will be surprised at how many different services are available to consumers. Salespeople are all motivated by commission. They get paid when you buy or sell. Motivation and compensation are a huge factor.

Model Home and Builder Agents. These agents are usually at the model in the neighborhoods they are selling. They can be Realtors or agents/brokers. The biggest difference is what they do and who they represent. These professionals work for the builder/seller. Most do <u>not</u> work for you as a buyer when you walk in the door. They are looking out for their boss, the guy that can fire them. You sign a contract that explains they work for the seller. They are not obligated to represent your interest, help you compare prices or advise you in any way.

Most if not all of them don't or are not allowed to sell other properties, so they do not have motivation to tell you about any other home available for sale. They are motivated by the product they have to sell.

They know the product they are selling very well, and are very helpful with the details of the home. They work to keep their product and contracts in a positive light.

Real Estate Consultants/Advocates: Consultants and Advocates educate consumers regarding their situation and options in real estate. They can, but don't always serve as the sales person. They help you determine if buying or selling is right for you. The advantage of a consultant is the ability to give you advice that is not motivated by a specific transaction or a specific sales person. They provide education and help the consumer find the best possible sales people to work with for the type of property they would like to buy or sell. They have access to salespeople who specialize in every type of real estate and can provide actual performance statistics from the MLS system to help the consumer choose wisely.

As an illustration look at the motivation differences in all types of real estate people. A model agent is motivated to have you buy one of the lots/homes their boss owns either in the development they are located in or another one the builder is working on. This is a limited part of the market. An agent or a realtor is motivated by you buying or selling anything they can help you with. It is not limited to a builder or a neighborhood and is only limited to the type of properties they work with and the location they work in. This represents a large part of the market.

A consultant is motivated by you buying or selling any property with any agent or realtor they help you find. This is any type of property, in any location, throughout the whole market. They are motivated by your success whatever that may be. They don't have to sell you a specific thing at all, but earn money by helping you find the best possible solution.

Real Estate Street Smarts

It is possible to have this help with no additional cost, because the consultant is paid a portion of the commission from the salesperson that you choose to help you buy or sell. Sales people are happy to pay the referring consultant. The sales people make the majority of the commission. A win-win for everyone involved.

Great consultants and salespeople will help you understand when the timing is wrong to buy or sell. Are they motivated by what is best for you and your family or are they pushing what will be best for them now?

Long-term business is built on a relationship of trust between the consumer and the professional.

Appraisers: Appraisers work for the lender or an individual depending on the situation. When there is a loan for part of the purchase, appraisers are hired by the lender to provide a report showing the value of a given property at a specific date with current market values. These values are determined by the opinion of the appraiser based on the comparison of the subject property to current sold homes that are similar. They must follow the rules and regulations that guide them as to the properties they choose and the adjustments they make for differences. This evaluation is done to give the bank an idea how much risk they assume with the loan they give to the buyer. The report shows the market trends and considers available competition to evaluate the risk for the lender.

At the time of service appraisers are paid a fee that is usually $400, give or take, for a full appraisal. They also have what we call a drive by appraisal where they do not go inside the home. This is a little less expensive. Appraisers may offer different pricing for just looking up sold comparables online, without seeing the home, and giving you an estimated value based on the what you tell them about the home. This would be an inexpensive way to get an idea of whether you should move forward with your plans to refinance or sell. You are basically paying for their time. This can save you a large portion of the fee if you don't know if your value is high enough for a purchase or refinance. If the value looks good, you would then move forward with a full appraisal that can be used for a loan. Real estate sales people will pull comparable sales for you for free as part of their service to you.

The motivation of an appraiser is not your purchase price. They get paid whether or not the price is what you wanted or regardless of whether or not your home sells. They can lose their license if they appraise homes in a fraudulent way that would mislead lenders as to the value of the home. The bank pays for their certified opinion of the value.

The pressure they feel is from the people who give them the work. Usually lenders, not one time sellers, are the ones who put pressure on them because these lenders send them many orders for appraisals. If the lender does not like their "performance" (appraised price) they may not send them more work. They can also be influenced by real estate professionals who want the price to come in to get the deal done. New federal appraisal rules require separation from the lender working on the loan and the appraiser.

Home inspectors: Home inspectors vary in services they offer and in cost. Their job is to help their customer understand the condition of the home. Everything from significant problems like a problem with the structure or a problem with a major system in the home to very miner things like a broken cover plate on an electrical outlet. Many of them will also provide information about maintenance and other helpful information like life expectancy of the systems of the home, such as the water heaters, home heating, cooling systems and appliances. The report they provide makes a great checklist for the owner to keep up the home and safeguard their investment.

Their cost is usually based on the size of the home. You can easily spend 300 to 400 dollars. You can add specific tests such as radon gas, methamphetamines, lead-based paint, stucco, termites, asbestos, and electrical efficiency testing, which add to the cost, to give you an idea. They are paid at the time of service. Inspectors are motivated by the person who hired them and the person that referred them. Happy customers (realtors, buyers, and sellers) lead to more work and money in the future. No home is perfect, even a brand new one. It is a balancing act for inspectors to be affective in giving the buyer a proper perspective on the seriousness of the problems the home has while helping the buyer understand how the home compares to normal conditions so the buyer knows that canceling a contract over a few very miner items will only lead to another contract on another home with at least a few miner items. In chapter eight you will learn how to get your money's worth out of your home inspection during your evaluations period of your contract, prior to closing.

Attorneys: Real estate attorneys have a license to practice law, to create legal documents and advise clients in legal matters. This is different from a real estate sales person who is licensed and authorized to fill out and advise clients on state authorized legal contracts regarding real estate. In most cases, attorneys are not motivated by you buying or selling. They are paid for their time. They do not have the risk of making nothing if you decide to change your plans. Usually this means you pay as you go at an hourly rate. If an attorney agrees to be paid in a manner similar to the commission structure of a real estate sales agent their motivation could change as it affects them differently. Some attorneys are also Realtors or sales agents. Attorneys are more common for high dollar and complex real estate transactions.

These are the major players in the real estate game. You might not use all of them. There are other professionals such as geologists, surveyors, city, and county workers, and others that you may work with to buy or sell a home. You will be better off if you understand where they are coming from and treat them how you would like to be treated.

Real Estate Street Smarts

-Chapter 4-
Determine The Market Value Of Your Home.
Get The Most Money Out Of Your Home By Pricing It Right!
And Don't Pay Too Much For Your Home As A Buyer!

Understanding your <u>local</u> real estate market is the key to correctly pricing your property along with understanding your specific needs regarding the sale. **Your situation and motivation, as the seller, affects the price of real estate**. Pricing correctly for your situation will bring you the best price.

First you must **evaluate your needs as a seller**. How soon do you need to sell your home? Do you have 2 weeks, 4 months, or is 2 years more accurate? Do you <u>want</u> to sell or really <u>need</u> to sell? The shorter the time you have to sell the lower your price will need to be to attract a buyer. The logic is simple. The lower the price, the more buyers that will be interested and the higher demand for the property. The target price is the highest possible price for the time you have to sell. This is determined by evaluating your current local market as it is always changing.

Why are you selling? Is there anything motivating you more than how much money you make from the sale of the home? It is best to think of the sale of your home as a business transaction and limit the amount of emotion involved. It is helpful to identify any needs you have from the sale of your home. What is your monthly cost if you do not sell? Time, money, or otherwise. Is the home vacant, or do you live in the home?

If your motivation to sell is because you would like a more convenient location to work, but your current situation is fine you will make more money from the sale of your home. You are not in a rush. What if you are in a rush? Maybe you have a life changing event with employment, health, or family. When you have to sell in a short period of time you will make less from your home.

You may change from a "seller with plenty of time" to a "seller in a hurry". If you fall in love with the next house before you sell your old house you will not make as much on your home. You may want to wait to look seriously until you have an accepted contract from a buyer on your current home.

If you decide to buy the new home before selling the old home you could become a super motivated seller as you may have significant unwanted monthly expenses. In this situation, pricing above market will waste a lot of your money as most of your costs are interest charges, taxes and insurance premiums that you do not get back. Only a small portion is principle, paying down your loan.

You will price the home differently if you have plenty of time to sell the home and are not losing money on the property each month. Timing is a great motivator for both buyers and sellers. If you only want one house, it is wise to sell your home before you buy your next home. You will make less if you have to sell quickly. Whenever possible avoid being a super motivated seller.

You also need to determine if you will repair and/or upgrade the home prior to selling. Or will you sell the home and property "as-is"? Much like detailing a car before you sell it to get a better price. Preparing your home for sale is well worth the time and money spent. Buyers will estimate the cost of work needed to be done on the high side. Homes that are clean and in good repair sell faster and for more money. If making repairs and preparing the home are not an option, adjust for that when you price your home. Homes sell in any condition, but for what price?

You need a buyer.

There are two general types of buyers. The "best house for us" buyers, and the "best deal for us" buyers. Some buyers are a mixture of the two. The first is concerned mostly with getting the right location, size, layout, amenities, etc. and wants a fair price. The second is looking primarily for a great price on a home that will meet their needs.

The second is more picky on price and less picky on the details of the house. The first is motivated by the house and is less concerned about the price of the home. As you can imagine, you can sell your home for more to a buyer who sees more value in the details of the home and how the home meets their needs than you would to the person primarily focused on a good price on your house or on another house, whichever.

If you are priced at or a little above market, the "right house" buyer will take a look at you, but the "deal buyer" will not. Although, if you have been on the market for many months they may come and make you a horribly low offer. If you are priced at a good value you will have all types and variations of buyers coming to see your home.

Establish Current Market Value In Three Ways.

1 **Compare SOLD homes.** You will know what price is best when you evaluate the market data. Start with the sold homes that appraisers are allowed to use to appraise your home for the buyers loan. These are homes that are within a few miles of your home, the closer the better. They need to be of similar location, size, age, style, level of finish, property type, lot size, and amenities. They need to have sold within the last six months.

Real Estate Street Smarts

Adjustments for differences need to be made to give you an accurate estimated value based on the comparison. Homes are so very different, even in neighborhoods with the same layout. Homes are not like other products such as cars that you can check the make, model, and condition, then simply look in a blue book for the price. Homes, even of the same layout, have differences inside and out as every one has a different idea of what makes a house a home.

The more adjustments that are made the more room for error in the evaluation. The best comparables are the ones that need little adjustment. You want comparables as similar to your property as possible. As close to the number of bedrooms, bathrooms, garages, etc. as you can.

Comparing differences.

Location: Buyer's appeal varies from city to city, from neighborhood to neighborhood, and even within a neighborhood. Proximity to jobs and other things that people need like shopping, schools, library, transportation (airport, bus routes, train routes etc.) and other amenities. It is vital that you get as close on this factor as you can, as it will affect value more than anything else. Areas with many conveniences, good schools, hospitals, shopping, and entertainment will be appealing to more buyers.

Comparables from the same neighborhood, when possible are best. You will need to make adjustments for differences. Sometimes you will need to make an adjustment even in the same neighborhood. For example, if your home is in a cul-de-sac or dead-end street with little traffic or noise and the home you are comparing is on a feeder street (busy street feeding traffic to other quiet streets) or a home that has an active train track bordering the yard, you will make a price adjustment for the difference. From the ideal location to the less appealing location an adjustment of 10% should be about right.

It is a simple fact that a buyer will not pay the same price for both locations. If they have the choice of either location at the same price they will pick the most ideal location.

The adjustment would be less if you are comparing a cul-de-sac to a normal non-feeder street that would only have local traffic. Likewise if you are comparing the home next to the train tracks to a home one street over from the train tracks you might only adjust 2 percent for the difference. You can hear the train from the next street over but it doesn't shake your house like the home right next to the track.

Remember that even though home owners get accustomed to the noise and may not think it is a big deal, prospective buyers will not be accustomed to it.

Another factor is positioning on the lot. Is there room on the side for RV parking and back yard access? Does the home face North, South, East, or West? In your area what is best? In Utah South facing and West facing are best as the sun melts the snow in your driveway and front porch while the homes across the street have much more ice and snow to shovel. Another consideration is shade. West facing homes naturally have evening shade to enjoy, the downside is the heat exposure on the many front windows to the west. Views also come into play. You will have to evaluate the differences for your area.

Size: The size of the homes you are comparing need to be of the same category as your house. If your home is 2500 square feet all finished, you will want homes as close to the same size as they will have similar rooms and room sizes. The square footage of your home plus or minus ten to fifteen percent. For a 2500 square foot home, homes that are 2200 to 2800 square feet would be best. Homes that are all finished or mostly finished are best.

By looking at your sold comparable homes, you will see how much buyers are willing to pay for the larger room size (same number of rooms, but larger size home) or additional rooms. You will also be able to see how much more they will pay for finished space. Remember most buyers would not be able to tell the difference between 2500 square feet and 2600 square feet. It is the function and use of each room, with the layout differences, that will be more important to the buyer.

Homes of a different size category should not be used as comparisons. The appeal of a home that is 3,500 square feet is so different than a 2,000 square foot home. Likewise a 5,500 square foot home would not be a good comparison for a 3,500 square foot home.

Age: The value of the improvements (house, shed, pool, etc.), not the land, goes down each year as it gets older. You must adjust for how old the home is. In our market $500-1000 per year difference is typical. You can check this in your area by comparing age and price differences on similar homes.

As a buyer if you had the choice of two similar homes but one home was 10 years newer (furnace, appliances, plumbing, electrical, all newer) how much more would you be willing to pay for the newer home? And don't forget the building code changes between the two and the design changes architects make to fit current lifestyles.

If I could point out an illustration of that for you it would have to be the popularity of garages and master suites. Two-car garages, master suites with walk-in closets and master bathrooms are standard in starter homes now and master suites are standard in most condos. Age definitely affects demand and price.

Real Estate Street Smarts

Interesting to me is that real estate or real property, they also call it, is referring to the land. The value of a mobile home, on land that you rent monthly, goes down each year just like a car or a motor home. It is the land that goes up in value in a balanced, or a sellers market.

Neighborhoods and developments go in cycles. As they get older they have a tendency to get more run down and less appealing from the curb. Appealing locations will get fixed up and improve. Some are even torn down to make room for new development. The appeal depends on the care and maintenance of the property by the home owner or the Home Owners Association. Run down neighborhoods attract less buyers.

Style: Rambler, two-story, split entry, multilevel, basement, mansion, modular, mobile on land, twin-home, and townhouse to name a few. There are different types of each of these styles as you can imagine. All homes by some degree are customized homes.

The use and feel of a home is different with the basic style of the home. Multi-level homes around the 2000 square foot size are very popular and effective. With this allocation of space you have a more open feel for the size of the home. It feels bigger than it is, because from your main level you can see the living room, kitchen, dining, family room, laundry room, and usually three or four bedrooms and two bathrooms.

On a rambler of the same size you would have the family room in the basement which makes a huge difference in the feel and use of the home. Larger ramblers have the living room, family room, kitchen, dining, two to four bedrooms, two or three bathrooms, and laundry on the main level. With a multilevel you get some of the bigger feel but you get to go up or down half a flight of stairs going from room to room. This is great if you like the exercise.

If at all possible use the same style to compare to your home. If this is not possible try to find the closest thing to it. This is done best by looking at the number of levels and the number of square feet on each level. A great example of close but not the same is a rambler and a split entry. A split entry is a rambler layout with half of the basement out of the ground, and the front door is located in the stairway between upper level and the bottom level. Ramblers sell for more because people don't like to do stairs every time they come in or out of the home. One advantage of the split entry is the increased daylight in the basement. When using another style make adjustments for the difference.

Level of finish: There are many things you can call upgrades, most of which are items you can see while you walk through the finished product, but it starts well before that with the type of construction. 2x4 walls, 2x6 walls or concrete insulated walls. The selections made for all the major systems of the home, heating, air conditioning, hot water systems, air purification, water purification, electrical, plumbing etc..

The basic categories are affordable, semi-custom, custom, and custom estate. There are great neighborhoods in each of these categories. Affordable homes which are usually known by the similar design of each home in the neighborhood. When it was new the buyers usually would be able to pick the house plan from a small list, then they would pick their color and type of product options from a small list. When you drive through these neighborhood you can see the same plans repeated.

In affordable new neighborhoods the builder commonly orders in bulk and sometimes saves even more cost by ordering a discontinued color or product from their supplier. As you can guess when you need one shingle or one piece of siding finding a match can be a bit of a problem.

Semi-custom homes give the buyer more options and selections to choose from. Usually this is a much longer list of floor plans, with a few variation options that can be made to the plan inside and outside to change the look. The quality of the materials for the homes in the neighborhood are higher-end than the affordable. As you drive through this neighborhood you can see the same plan but it does not look exactly the same because of the variations to the front elevation (changes to front design). In this category you can have a large range of products to choose from for the inside. From affordable finish to Luxury finish. Most buyers will pick items in the middle to match the level of finish in the neighborhood.

Custom homes are designed for the buyers needs and taste. In a custom neighborhood the homes generally do not look alike. Each home was built for a specific lifestyle, taste, and need. The Builder and/or buyer select every item that goes into the home. The home usually has middle grade to luxury finish items and features. They are unique to their own design and usually have many extras and upgrades.

Custom estate homes stand out because of their size, both of the land and the home. Their luxurious quality and workmanship also make them stand out. There are many amenities inside and outside of the home. The have rooms that most people would only dream of: indoor pools, indoor basketball or tennis courts, dance rooms, libraries, and grand open spaces. Outdoor features that are only limited by the owners imagination. Many of these neighborhoods are gated offering privacy and security to the residents.

There is an obvious difference in the materials used in each of these categories. The cost from one category to another is very different. You must compare homes from the same category.

With the homes in your category compare the level of finish differences by reviewing what finish items they have listed. A few examples are central vacuum system, intercom system, alarm system, smart house system (control the systems of your house from remote location on the computer), theater room/systems, moldings, cabinets, flooring type, paint, countertops, appliances, lighting, fireplaces, landscaping features, pools, spas, etc.

The level of finish usually matches the type of home. This is not always true as some basic homes have high end finishes and some large homes have inexpensive finishes. A basic finished home would likely have laminate countertops, vinyl and carpet flooring, small and limited molding, one tone paint, basic cabinet design (in the most affordable wood options for the time), 2x4 walls, orange peel texture and only basic systems for the home.

When comparing remember that if it has upgrades it will be mentioned. By reading the marketing remarks about the property you can tell what type of finish the home has. If they have granite countertops, or a double oven in a gourmet kitchen, they are definitely going to tell you all about it.

The key with level of finish is to recognize what category the home is in so you make correct comparisons. Tile flooring lasts longer than vinyl and is worth more to a buyer. In the sold data you will see how the level of finish affects how much more a buyer will pay for nicer items in the home.

Buyers like to see what they expect or to be surprised by something a little nicer than the norm for the market they are in. If the homes you are competing against have a higher end finish than your home, you must compensate with your price to attract buyers.

Property type: PUD Planned Unit Development's differ from a typical single family home because they get to play by different rules. Lot size may look, on paper, to be very small because the front yard and the back yard are owned by the HOA and are maintained by the HOA (most cases). The streets could be smaller and also owned and cared for by the HOA. Usually they come with other amenities for the community such as a pool, park, club house, walking trails, etc.. Not having to mow your lawn and having access to all the fun stuff does not come for free. Always notice the monthly HOA fees advertised. This is usually a considerable amount. If the HOA is doing a good job the whole neighborhood will look great.

Some developments are not PUD's but do have a master plan for the community with an HOA to enforce rules and regulations for the neighborhood and usually they maintain common area such as parks, walking trails etc.. In these neighborhoods each owner takes care of their own property. The HOA is the enforcer. If they do it well, the whole neighborhood will look good for the benefit of all. HOA fees are significantly less as their cost and amenities are less.

A single family home without Covenants Conditions & Restrictions (CC&R's) is the right choice for the person that does not want anyone telling him or his neighbor what to do with his property. It can be good, or bad. The downside of this freedom is that everyone has a different idea of what is good and what is not. For this reason HOA enforcing CC&R's have become very popular in new subdivisions.

Twin-homes can be any of the above mentioned types with HOA fees and without, just remember the adjoining or shared wall makes these a type all of their own. Townhouses with their neighbors on the sides, and condo's with neighbors up, down, and side to side. Townhouses and Condo's will have HOA fees.

With Townhouses remember the difference between an end-unit (only one connected neighbor and more windows) and a middle-unit with neighbors on each side and not as many windows.

With Condo's which level they are on will affect the demand. Top level condo's will sell for more and usually have more amenities with them. Don't forget if you are on top you don't have neighbors above you.

The same neighborhood is best for property comparisons. It is critical to know the demand and appeal of the development when there is significant HOA involvement. A poorly managed HOA will lower appeal and demand for the properties in it. If you use comparables that are in the same neighborhood under the same HOA the comparison will be accurate. If the comparable property has a different HOA an evaluation of the two HOA's is necessary.

When comparing properties with an HOA check what is included in the HOA fees. Some will include Cable or Satellite TV, high speed Internet, RV parking, Horse Property, tennis courts, weight rooms, playgrounds, swimming pools etc.. The possibilities are endless.

Lot Size: There are 43,560 square feet in an acre of land. Most homes are not on an acre, they are on a portion of an acre. The most common way we describe the lot size is by the portion of an acre, 1/4 acre (.25 acres) or sometimes it is by the square foot measurement (.10 acres) 4,356 square feet. (I guess that sounds better than a tenth of an acre).

When you can, you want compare homes with similar lot sizes. Land is valuable and in high demand. The small lots (.05) 1/20th of a acre (usually the footprint of the building in a PUD), 1/10th of a acre (.1 acres) would be a small home with small yard, 1/4th of an acre (.25 acres), 1/3rd of an acre (.33 acres), 1/2 of an acre (.5 acres) are all different categories of residential lots. .5 to 1 acre lots are more typical for Estate Homes and homes in the country. You don't' want to compare a one acre parcel with a quarter acre or a third as they are completely different. You can compare the quarter to the third with an adjustment for the extra space. The same for third to half. You would not want to make adjustments from a 1/10 to 1/2 acre lot because they are so different.

For properties with large acreage. Adjustments for 5 to 10 acres or 10 to 80 acres are very big. The use and value for the property can be so different. With large parcels like farms, the land itself becomes a major market comparison all on its own. Land should be compared to land with a similar use to establish a per acre price. These properties can have many improvements that add value. Water rights, water shares, wells, equipment, and structures are just a few items that add value to the property. For most people it will just be a regular residential lot.

On small lots, the shape and placement of the home on the lot can be as important as the actual size of the lot. Most people enjoy back yard space over any other part of their property. Large front yards and side yards are less useful for most people as they are less private and convenient.

Amenities: Anything of value to a buyer could be an amenity. A hard thing to remember is that buyers have different ideas of what is valuable and what is not. The key to making money on your amenities is to wait for a buyer who sees the value in your chosen amenities. A good example of this is a pool. For some this is the most wonderful addition you could make to a property, but for others it is the worst possible use of the space and is seen as a serious liability.

Some items will be generally valued, like a fenced yard, or shade trees. The view from the home inside and out are also a factor. On a residential street, located on a hillside, the homes on the view side of the street (back of home faces view, usually with the amenity of a walk-out basement) sell for much more than the other side of the same street. In most cases the homes across the street have elevated driveways that can be steep and difficult to access the garage. Their views are more of their private hillside than the valley, and the homes typically have a normal basement instead of a daylight or walk-out basement. The feel of the homes are different even when it is the same house plan.

Homes usually are designed with the family rooms, kitchens, dining rooms, and master bedrooms off the back of the home. This is ideal for the view or to watch the kids. It is possible that a builder or home owner would design a home specifically for the lot and the view. If they did, it would be mentioned in the remarks so you would know they had many view windows out the front of the home. In this situation an adjustment would be made from the home across the street but it would be half of what the adjustment would have been. A smart builder or owner will design their home for the location they are in to maximize the benefits of the lot. It doesn't cost a lot more to do and will add value to the property.

Other amenities to consider are: decks, covered decks, patios, covered patios, vegetable gardens, flower gardens, green houses, hot tubs, saunas, playgrounds, sport courts, barbeque pits, swimming pools, outdoor lighting, water features, walkways, and any upgrade item that is not typical for the type of property. Even sidewalks, curbs and gutters could be in this category if they are not the norm.

The point: You need to have a knowledge of the differences between the properties you are comparing and your home, so you can be accurate in your assessment of how the buyer will perceive the value of your home. This is an important point so I will repeat that it is important to see how buyer's will perceive the value of your home.

It does not matter how much you think your home is worth. You don't want your home anymore--remember? I am kidding a little on that one. Seriously though you need to remember that for a buyer to make an offer on your home they need to see the value in it. If your price is too high they may not even consider looking at it. If they can get the same house for 40,000 less and put 15,000 into the home to make it like yours…. They will do the math, make sure you do the math as well.

When you are analyzing these sold homes take a look at their market history. You can get this from your agent. How many days did it take to sell? Did they start at a higher price and then lower their price, or did they leave it the same? Did they make other changes that would affect the marketing of the home?

When the homes sold can impact your evaluation. A home that sold two weeks or a month ago is better than five or six months ago. The more current the better, but work with what you have.

2 Check properties that are Under Contract:

Step two is to evaluate the under contract properties. This is done the same way you compare the sold homes, but how you value the data is a little different.

These are properties for sale that have accepted an offer from a buyer to purchase the property. You will not know how much the buyer is willing to pay or what the terms of the contract are. But we do learn one important thing about the property. They, at their listed price, attracted a buyer willing to make them an offer that they accepted. This is a great point of reference because you want to sell your house, not just have it on the market.

These homes are not sold so the value you put on the comparison is not solid for a selling price, but more of an indicator if your listed price is good. In many cases the sold price is less than the listed price--in every market except for a sellers market this is the case. In a seller's market the high buyer demand and the low supply of homes create a frenzy of buyer competition for each home: which drives offer prices to match or exceed the list price as buyers try to get the home.

So, if you are planning your real estate life, a bit of advice you might find funny... Buy in a buyer's market and sell in a seller's market. If you had complete control of your timing that would be great, wouldn't it?

In a heavy buyer's market or declining market, the prices will be falling so under contract and active homes can be offered for less than homes that sold in the last six months.

The under contract homes you look at should include all style types and any year built that are similar in size to your home. This way you see what is moving in the market. Play close attention to list price compared to the sold homes. Are prices going up or down, or are they staying about the same. The key is to know what is going on in your market, which brings us to our next step.

3 Last but not least, compare Active homes FOR SALE.

Also known as your competition for those precious buyers. Look at all styles of homes in a list from least expensive to most expensive, just like a buyer would. With the actives, you don't want to look at homes just like yours at first. Start with an open search in a large price range that includes all property types. Focus more on how much a buyer has to spend on a house. From your research on the sold and under contract homes, you have an idea what your price should be. Search well under and above the suggested price to see what the competition is. You will find out what the current market requires to get it done.

As you go through the list, review the details of each home comparing your home to it as you go. Make a note of your opinion on whether it is a more expensive property, less expensive, or about the same value as your home. As you do this, you will find a point in the list where your home would be the best value to a buyer. You want the point where the highest price meets best value. Meaning that if a buyer wants the best deal in your homes market you would be it, or at least priced the same as the best value.

Value to the buyer is determined by comparing the location, size, age, style, level of finish, property type, lot size, and amenities. The word VALUE is important because you will not be pricing the same as a bank-owned home or distressed home that is sold as-is. Even though the price on these homes are lower, the value may not be, because of the work involved to get them looking like your home.

As an example, a home just like yours is priced $10,000 less than the price you have picked. You are still the better value because your house is located in a cul-de-sac and has an extra garage. You know that the value of the garage and location are worth more than $10,000 to a buyer, making you the better value.

After you make note of the price-point you would need to be at from this search, do another search of properties very close to what you have. Search by what makes your property stand out. Does it have a large lot, horse property, cul-de-sac, 3-car garage? Or maybe it is four bedrooms and three full baths because you noticed most homes on the first active search have only two bathrooms. What makes the home stand out?

On this search go through the same process in picking the most logical price point. Compare the two active pricing points. Are they the same or could you possibly make more on your home if you wait for someone who wants exactly what you have? In a depreciating market, pricing to be the best value for a buyer will get your home sold. If that price is not going to work for you, and you want to be more in the average listed price range, be prepared to be patient and remember your plan. You can always lower your price later if you want to speed up the process.

It is best to start with the price buyers will like and stick with it. When a home is first listed on the MLS system buyers and agents are notified of the new listing. If your home fits their criteria they will take a look. If your price is too high you risk missing the buyers search criteria or risk the buyers dismissing you as an over priced property. No one wants to overpay for their home.

Keep in mind the offer you receive usually is lower than your list price. If you are fortunate and have more than one offer, full price becomes a likely possibility.

In a balanced market, list prices will be a little higher than sold comparables. The sold price most likely would be a little under list price. In a seller's market the list price is on the high end of the sold comparables and multiple offers from the high demand and limited supply provide the seller with full price offers and even offers above the listed price. A word of advice. Don't spend the money mentally or physically. The home has to appraise and successfully close before the money is yours. Getting the appraisal to come in at your price can be difficult in a sellers market. Sometimes buyers will offer much higher than the listed price to make sure they get the house instead of another competing buyer. With the thought that the home will not appraise at the offer price and they will be able to get the price down.

If you want a good indicator of how your market is, take the number of active homes in your neighborhood, town, or county and compare it with the number of sold homes and under-contract homes.

If there are 20 homes available as actives, 1 home under contract, and 10 homes sold in the last 12 months, you have a 2-year supply of homes if no one else decides it is their time to sell.

If there are 20 homes available, 6 homes under contract, and 60 homes sold in the last year, you will know with this 4-month supply of homes that your home will likely sell quickly and at a high price.

If you are in a depreciating buyer's market with many homes for sale and few buyers, you must remember to price aggressively. The best deals will sell, but during these times they end up being the only homes that sell. If you must sell in this market situation, remember, time is money. Prices will be lower three months from now. You can end up chasing the market down lowering your price but never being the best value on the market.

In a stable or increasing market the active homes will be priced at or above the sold homes.

The Key to Success!

Your price should be appealing to buyers when they compare your home with the other homes available on the market and your price should also fit within the estimated value the sold homes suggest. Most buyers get a loan, so even if you could get a buyer to want your home at a price above the sold comparables it would not appraise that high and their loan will be based on the appraised value.

Think like a buyer! How do they see your home? What you don't want to hear from a buyer is "This place better have Gold Toilets at this price." When you price too high you are simply helping the competition look good and you help the buyer decide on someone else's home.

If you decide your strategy is to go for the highest price and that the money is more important than the timing or speed of the sale, just remember to be patient with the time it takes and your real estate agent, if you have one, because all the advertising in the world won't get an over-priced home to sell quickly. You will be fishing for the buyer that wants exactly what you have. They will pay more because they value what you have more than the typical buyer. Sometimes you get your fish quickly and sometimes the fish you're looking for has not decided to move yet. So be patient and realize that even the perfect buyer for your home does not want to overpay. The value needs to be there even when the match seems to be perfect.

Where can I get the comparable data that I need? The active homes for sale you compete against will be all over the Internet. You can look at homes all over the United States that are currently for sale. Realtors (members of the National Association of Realtors) post their listed homes for sale on a Multiple Listing Service (MLS). Realtors use this service to help each other sell the homes listed and offer on the MLS a commission to other agents for bringing the buyer.

The local MLS in your area usually is automatically loaded to a public website for all to see. It is also loaded onto **www.realtor.com** (on this site you can see homes all over the U.S.). It is limited in information to the public and only contains active properties.

Each state in the U.S. will either be a disclosure state or a non-disclosure state. Utah is a non-disclosure state. In these states the sold price of property is not recorded on public records.

To get the information you need you will want to ask a Realtor to send you the active, under-contract and sold homes within the criteria you decide on. The Realtor can email the list to you. Tell them what information you want, including any statistics you would like to evaluate.

I would ask for a market summary report for active, under-contract and sold homes (this shows the number of homes in the different price ranges). This will help you see the supply and demand generally. Also ask for a Sales-Per-Month report (this will help you determine buyer demand and seasonal trends. This is helpful in deciding what time to sell). If they have a quarterly comparison ask for that as it shows trends over the last few years for days on market, property values, and supply and demand. You can also ask them their opinion on what additional information would be helpful for you.

Most agents will provide this information for free if they are going to be considered for the job of selling your home, if you decide to sell. When you call you may not know if selling is right for you. Agents know this. They are usually willing to send the information to you so that you can evaluate your situation. If you decide to hire an agent to sell your home, give them an opportunity to interview. You may already have an agent you like. If you do, call them, after all they probably like you as well and will be willing to help. Don't demand a lot of their time. Be honest and upfront with them. You don't need them to drive out to meet with you at first. If you explain that you are just starting to check into the possibility of a housing change, you will find that they are very helpful and don't expect you to know right away if moving is right for your situation. After you evaluate the situation you may want more of their time.

Some agents will want to meet with you in person. This is smart for them to do so. It is an opportunity for them to meet a person likely to be in the market soon. If this is the situation, let them know that you will require time to evaluate the market data after they bring it to you. They should respect that. If they don't I would move on.

If you know of a home in your area that has sold without a Realtor you can ask the buyer or the seller of the property about the terms of the sale. If you want to use the comparable for an appraisal get a copy of the settlement statement to give the appraiser. With permission, Title Companies can get them for the appraiser. Don't be surprised if the details of the sale are a little different. Many sellers will tell their neighbors the gross price of the sale and forget to mention the concessions they paid for the buyer, like closing costs or incentives, that actually lower the amount of the seller's net sales price. Appraisers, Realtors, and you as the seller should be looking at the net sales price (sales price minus concessions).

Trust but verify. If you meet with an agent it is smart to get their estimation on your homes value. It should be a valued opinion. Review the active, under contract, and sold homes from the Multiple Listing Service for your area. You want the data from the source. Realtors have a code of ethics and rules in their local MLS to keep the information as accurate as possible.

If an agent gives you a market analysis make sure it contains the reports on each home they are comparing to. This way you can look at their adjustments to see if you agree with the estimation.

Adjustments can be made so the report shows any range of value. This is done by changing the adjustment values. A simple example is the appreciation from a sold home. It calculates the time from the sale to the current day and how much more the home would be worth at the current rate of appreciation. By changing this from two to eight percent the suggested value of each home will go up.

Each category gives the opportunity to change and adjust the value at which the adjustments are made. This is why an original of the actual home data is important. Use common sense to come up with your own opinion of how buyers will interpret the value of your home.

Use the active homes method of comparison to evaluate any price an agent gives you. If you put your home on the market at that price will the home be competitive? It is worth your time educating yourself on the market so that you know what price is right. You will be armed with the facts and reality when you talk with professionals.

You will know if an agent gives you a price that is obviously low or high. The agent is either dishonest or inexperienced. Either way you do not want them.

You want the agent that is looking out for your best interest.

Evaluate their motivation. If the agent is looking out for you they would not suggest a price that is well under the necessary price point for your timing needs, but if they are thinking about themselves they may want your price to be low so they can sell your home very quickly and get paid quickly then move on to the next deal. It is your money we are talking about giving away for a speedy sale. If it is because of your need to sell in two weeks then the agent is doing their job.

If they suggest going more than ten percent below current market you may want to agree to a higher amount with price reductions every two to three days to get it done and make as much money as you can.

There are many investor companies that are looking for homes to buy at a twenty to thirty percent discount. That can be done very quickly. You can use logic to evaluate how much you would need to come down for your timing needs.

An agent that is looking out for your best interests would not suggest a price that is too high for your timing needs. But if they are worried more about getting the listing than they are about you, they might. We call this "buying the listing" when agents give the seller an unrealistic value well above the current honest and fair market value. They do not provide accurate market data that supports the value, they simply tell people what they want to hear.

Most people like the idea of more money so they get the listing. Agents do this knowing that they will have to get the price down later to get the home sold. During this time they can pick up buyers, from the sign and other marketing, that they can help buy other homes that are not overpriced and make even more money. When the home is not selling they get the seller to lower the price.

The point here is that they waste your time and money having you on the market at the wrong price, and they get paid to sell your home at the price the honest agent suggested.

The agent you want is the one that provides you with honest information with the intent to educate you and then let you decide what you want to do. These agents are motivated by your best interests and are truly valuable.

Pricing your home correctly for your required timing is the most important part of the marketing. If the home is priced incorrectly, it will not appeal to anyone in their right mind, and most people are smart, especially when it comes to their own money.

If you are selling your home on your own your market knowledge will give you the confidence you need in your home's value when a professional is negotiating with you for the best interests of the buyer.

Either way you use this knowledge you win. Knowledge is power. Knowledge will make you more money. It is your money, you've earned it!

Pricing strategy. At last you have your price. Now one more thing to think about. Do you price your home at an even amount? Say $200,000. Or $199,500, or $198,788. Many Internet sites have drop down windows to select the price range. If the price you are considering is at a common price point like $200,000 the home will pull up for searches with $200,000 selected as the minimum price or the maximum price. The result is more views on the Internet. If the price you have is $210,000 this advantage is not there. Most sites have the windows at $200,000 to $225,000.

Buyers tend to buy at the top of their price range. Showing up earlier on the list the buyer is viewing can be an advantage. At $199,500 you will be seen before the evenly priced 200k price. There is a psychological difference in the pricing, somehow this price seems to be a lot less when it is only $500 different.

Another strategy is to price just under a common price point with a price that looks to be calculated with exactness. The $198,788 looks like it was calculated. You would not just pick a number like that. Because it is over 1,000 less than the 200k price point the home will come up well before the evenly priced home.

You can argue for any type of pricing strategy. If your price is close to a major price point on Internet drop down windows I would use it. If your price is not a major price point look at the competition to see which homes you can come in front of if you price at an exact price that will stand out like the $198,788 example. If you do not want to go with that strategy you can come in front of many homes by going with a $199,400 or if you want you can try all 3 strategies by simply changing your price. When you change your price you will pop up on new listing notification that agents and buyers use, and that is a good thing.

Typo's happen. First check the price on the Internet. A typo here would make it so you wouldn't pull up on searches. Other categories are equally important. These small oversights by agents, owners, or staff members are unintentional but

---

FOOD FOR THOUGHT

Price can fix any problem! Every home can sell if the price is right! If you are having a hard time selling your home take a step back and look at your home again. Is there a reason buyers are driving by but not making an appointment to see the inside? Missing shingles on your roof from a strong wind? Unsightly exterior? Is the marketing entered correctly? If you find no mistakes on the marketing, and can find nothing about the home that needs to be improved it is time to change your price.

have a large impact. Go online when your home is posted and double check the listing data. Check the map links for accuracy. The more accurate the better.

If your timing is short and you are not getting showings or offers, lower the price by two to five percent every two to three weeks until you have an offer. You need to give it a little time, but not too long. If buyer demand is very low in your market, price the home to be the best value and think of what buyers like and make special offers. For example paying the buyer's closing costs for them or including an item they would like to have. A washer and dryer can be very helpful to a first time homebuyer. Who is your likely buyer and what would they like? The more you think like a buyer the better off you will be. Buyers drive the market.

Talk with a professional before you make a decision and get started. Markets change as they are affected by many factors. Supply and demand can change for many reasons. The availability of home loans, interest rates, government regulations, and tax codes to name a few. You need to consult with a professional to get the most current information. If the rules are in the process of changing, it can and will change the motivation of buyers and sellers. To show you an example. The government could remove any one of the benefits of home ownership and home investment. If Uncle Sam removed or reduced the capital gains tax on investment property it would make selling more appealing.

However, if Uncle Sam added a sales tax to real estate transactions it would make it less appealing to sell to everyone with the increased cost (this is an idea that comes up from time to time. You can thank the National Association of Realtors for lobbying against it).

Another example to help you understand how things, that you may not see, can affect you, if a developer/builder has a project pending it can flood the supply of the type of property you have to sell. If the new homes available are the same price or a lower price, your home just went down in value. If you keep your price the same, not knowing about the new homes available at the same price, your home will likely sit without much attention to it.

If a large company has announced expanding or opening a new location the new jobs added will add to home buyer demand, and can completely change a local market. Things that you don't know (because you are not focused on it each day) affect you. Do the research or talk to someone locally that knows what is happening in your market.

Hiring a great real estate agent is the best way to increase your knowledge base. When you hire an agent they have the responsibility to look out for your best interest throughout the staging, marketing, negotiations, and settlement of your home.

Real Estate Street Smarts

A great agent with the skill set you need is crucial.

When you are the buyer you will use these same comparison methods to evaluate and come up with your own opinion of the value of the property.

The biggest mistakes buyers make is basing the value of the home by only comparing it to active homes that are in competition with the home they choose. And choosing a home without researching the other home choices available to them. As a buyer you should see at least ten homes either before you make an offer or at least during your evaluation period on your contract to buy the home you fell in love with.

Your opinion of the value as the buyer is what matters most. You should look at the comparable sold and under contract properties to determine what you should pay for your home.

Take advantage of the people who are there to help you. Read other articles and books to increase your knowledge. <u>Never take information from this book or other sources as a specific consultation directed to your situation</u>. The intent is to provide the concepts for your own knowledge and benefit. Seek council from those professionals you trust prior to buying or selling any property.

In a movie most kids enjoy, the character Edna Mode in Disney's <u>The Incredibles</u>, states and I quote **"Luck favors the prepared."** There are many professionals available to help you succeed. Realtors, Appraisers, lenders, Title Searchers, Escrow Officers, Home Inspectors, Surveyors, Geologists, City Officials, Accountants (CPA's), and Financial Planners. All can help you do the right thing for your situation.

-Chapter 5-
Do It Yourself Or Hire A Professional?

You will need to determine what is best for your own situation. After reading this book you will have a better idea of what it takes to get the job done. Do you have time to get the tasks done? Are you comfortable with the risks? It is important to be realistic while making your plans.

Many people want to try it on their own and if that does not work they will hire someone. The affect of this plan will depend on what the market is doing at the time and what you are doing to get the job done.

Of those that try to sell on their own, some are successful and some are not able to sell without the MLS and the help of a professional. There are individuals, builders and investors that prefer to do the work the agents do instead of hiring it out. This happens in most industries. It is common for someone to do their own taxes or put in their own floor. This is not a problem and should not be thought of as a problem for salespeople or consumers.

In my view it only becomes a problem if a consumer uses the services of a professional and does not pay them. If an installer put your floor in for you and you did not pay them they could put a lien on your house. If they did the work they should be paid. If they did a bad job you would need to work out a solution.

If you use a buyers agent, listing agent or a consultant treat them fairly. If they find your house, find you a buyer, or find you the right agent you should not go around them for your benefit or for the benefit of others. It is dishonest.

If you want to sell your home yourself, do it. If you know you don't want to hire a realtor be upfront with them. You can ask them to send comparables to you on email without taking a lot of their time. You can pay an appraiser to give you an appraisal to back up your own opinion of the value. If you have a friend they are likely happy to help you, just as they would if they knew how to fix your bathroom sink drain if it needed work.

Professionals should not mind at all that you want to do the work yourself to save money or because you want it done a certain way. They will not have to spend time or money on your transaction.

Much of the bad feelings in the real estate industry come from both professionals and consumers treating each other poorly. The industry would be much better off if consumers would think about how they would want to be treated if they were the professional and if professional would always treat consumers how they would like to be treated if they were the consumer. Selfishness on all sides causes unnecessary problems and pain.

Real Estate Street Smarts

What do you need to do?

If you are going to do it on your own you will be smart to look at what professionals do and put forth the same amount of effort into the job. This is the only way to get similar results.

It is much like a floor that was done by the homeowner. Some look just like a professional installed the floor. The value of the floor is the same as if a professional installed the floor because the homeowner did the research to know how to do it right.

I know you have seen a floor that a homeowner installed that did not turn out well. They did not know what they were doing. The floor looks bad and because of this the floor has no positive value to a buyer it actually has a negative value because the buyer will be ripping it out and putting a new floor in.

Do a good job. Don't cut corners. Don't assume that salespeople do nothing. Learn what they do and get to it and get it done. Pricing your home right, preparing your home for showings, ordering title work to check for problems, marketing the home, negotiating, and solving problems are all things you can do.

The question you have to ask yourself is do I have the knowledge, skills, and time to do what it takes to get my home sold? Will I get the best price or are homes selling for more on the MLS? If your sales price is increased ten percent higher by going through a Realtor and your increased cost is six percent, you would make four percent more. You will have to evaluate that for yourself. I have seen consumers with strong opinions on both sides of the debate.

If you decide to hire someone you will benefit from all they bring to the project. As you weigh your options I think it is wise to consider the protections you receive with a professional helping you. These are things you can also do for yourself with some work.

Selling a home, you will have a property condition disclosure signed by the buyer when you have an accepted contract. This protects you as a seller from a buyer who gets buyers remorse in the future and dreams up a lawsuit. Even many years after the sale, if the buyer can prove that you lied, covered up, or misrepresented the property to them and the judge agrees, you can end up with a financial disaster and stressful mess. By being open and honest on the disclosure, meaning telling the buyer what you know about the property, you protect yourself. By having the document signed by the buyer and dated it shows that they were told about an item before they purchased the home.

HOA, CC& R rules and fees properly disclosed to the buyer with documentation signed by the buyer is a must. Know about title problems: when to look, what to look for, and how to solve issues without putting you in breach of a contract with a buyer. How to protect your interest and accomplish what you want in your purchase contract.

You will need to know how to successfully negotiate with the other party, and what to do when you have appraisal problems without just giving up your money for the benefit of the buyer.

Utilize marketing to the masses. Everyone needs to know your home is for sale. Putt your home in the best light possible. Emphasize the positive without lying to a buyer. Know what to do with inspection items the buyer may ask for.

Avoid unnecessary risks with the property by not allowing buyers to move in until it is recorded and finished. The buyer may ask to move in during escrow, after you have a signed contract but before it is closed. Utilities need to stay on until after recording and buyers have been notified.

Understand the contract terms and implications. Know people who can take care of problems that come up during escrow in time for closing and avoid delays.

Have a secure environment for showings. Safeguard your family. Protect your family from personal harm, theft, identity theft, fraud and scammers. If you hire an agent you can ask about their E and O insurance that will help cover damages that resulted from a showing. Insurance varies so you would need to find out what is covered.

Check out the buyer before you are committed to a contract. Do they need a loan, are they qualified. Do they have a house to sell? Is it priced right for what it is? What conditions do you need to add or take off the contract for this buyer? How much earnest money should you require the buyer to put down?

It is also helpful to have an expert that spends everyday following local news and statistics that affect your local real estate market. They have a level of expertise because they spend so much more time involved in real estate related matters. If you want the same results you will need to do your homework.

Consider what agents can do for a buyer.

Inventory knowledge an agent has for the area they work in will help you get to know the areas that are developing and growing and areas that are declining and receding. You need to know what is going on in the neighborhoods you choose from. If the neighborhood is going down hill your enjoyment and investment will not go as well. Agents can help you find the information you need to make a decision.

Agents can help you know what is normal. What should I expect from the seller? Who pays for what? What is a must and what is okay either way?

What does the title report tell me? Are there any red flags? What are the problems we need to work through now and are there any potential problems for later?

Real Estate Street Smarts

Agents can help you find home inspectors, lenders, title companies, construction tradesmen, attorneys, geologists, surveyors, accountants, and other service providers related to the moving process.

A good agent will know the contracts well and will help you protect yourself and your earnest money. They can help you keep the deadlines of the contract. You must pay attention to the details to make sure you do not breach the contract or in any way make the contract invalid.

You don't want a money pit. Money pits can be from bad loans or bad properties. With a bad loan you will dump more money than you should into your housing much like a home that has many problems. These homes and loans require at one time, or on an ongoing basis, a large supply of money to keep the home livable and maintained.

Agents can help you have proper perspective as you evaluate homes. Know which things can be changed and which ones you will always have to live with. Some items cost too much to be changed much like you would not spend $5,000 to repair the engine and transmission of a car worth $2,000. It doesn't make financial sense. You buy a different car that does not need the work. Unless your parents built the car, then you may do it for sentimental reasons (a little of my bad sense of humor). At that point it is not about the money is it?

A great agent is priceless when you are negotiating for the best price, both at first when you make your offer and during your inspection period as you negotiate the second time after inspections are completed.

Agents can be very helpful explaining the process so you know what to expect and can plan the timing of your move and the many other details that go into moving. Understanding the paperwork and knowing what is going on and when things need to happen are very valuable.

The cost for a buyers agent can be free. They are not always but when the home you buy is on the MLS system the listing agent is offering a buyers agent part of the commission the seller is paying, so if the amount the seller is paying covers the amount on your buyer-broker agreement it can be totally free.

While they are not for everyone, many people feel the help of a professional, on the largest transaction of your life, is more valuable than the cost.

According to the National Association of Realtors homes sold by Realtors through the MLS sell for more than homes sold by private sellers. This is a general statement and should not be thought of as an absolute on every home. But I have seen the truth in this statement as I have listed and sold homes for more than they were listed for by the private seller just prior to going on the MLS.

Private sellers struggle with knowing what price the home should be listed for. Some price low and some high and a few price their home just right. The second biggest problem for private sellers is that not enough buyers in the market know they are for sale.

If you can put the effort in and have the knowledge needed you can be successful in your effort to sell or buy on your own. **Remember the floor installation, anyone can do the job themselves but not everyone can do it well!**

Real Estate Street Smarts

-Chapter 6-
How To Select The Best Real Estate Agent.

Real estate agents come in many varieties. In this chapter you will learn what to look for in an agent. Understanding the basics of the Multiple Listing Service they use, and the motivating factors they deal with each day give you the insight you need to select the right agent for your specific needs.

The right agent for you.
The agent you need will depend on what you have to sell. Agents work in many areas of real estate, but may specialize in certain property types or areas.

Some agents specialize in a geographic location whether it is a town, development, or county. Other agents specialize in property types like condo's, farm and ranch properties, new construction, investment properties, vacation and resort properties, residential homes, commercial properties, short sales, and bank REO's (real estate owned).

Agents don't make a habit of turning work down. You will do well by using an agent that specializes in what you have to sell. They will have more experience, knowledge, and connections that will be helpful to get the property sold.

The medical field is a great example of the benefits of specialists. If you need a brain surgeon you would not just ask for a doctor or even a surgeon, you want a specialist!

The challenges and problems are different for different property types. With a single family home located in a subdivision you would not have green belt, property tax recapture, and water share transfer issues like you might on a piece of farm land. Your results will be better when you work with someone that works with your specific property type and location.

Understand cost and value to be a smart shopper.
In other Industries you pay much more for a specialist. This is not the case in real estate. In many cases a brand new agent would be charging the same fee as the seasoned agent. An agent that is more generalized in their expertise would likely cost as much as an agent that is very specialized in their expertise. Real estate commissions are negotiable. Real estate brokerages can set pricing for their agents. Industry wide price fixing is not allowed. There are offices that will allow their agents to set their own pricing. Value is determined by comparing the benefit by the cost. A sales person that provides the product or performance you want at a good price. And lets not forget avoiding paying top dollar for a poor performance or product.

Real Estate Street Smarts

Factors that affect agents. It helps to understand how agents get paid and what different office types there are. Real estate brokerages are either a national franchise or a local company. The difference for the agent between the two is the franchise fee and franchise products. You could have a long debate on which type is best. The franchise provides national advertising for the brand, and provides programs the agents can use in their business.

Commission splits with the company and the agent can vary greatly--no matter if the company is a national franchise or not. Everything from a 50/50 split to 100 percent plans with a monthly fee or transaction fee (agent pays the monthly or transaction fee and keeps all the commission). With a split plan the agent keeps a portion and the company keeps a portion. As you can imagine if an agent is working for a national franchise office the franchise fee comes off the top. Most companies have more than one plan available for agents to choose from.

These companies compete for the agents much like the agents compete for your business. Companies that offer percentage splits often offer an increase in the percentage the agent keeps as the agents production level increases. 60% for the agent and 40% for the office is a common starting rate. A rate of 70%, 80%, or even 90% splits are common for seasoned agents.

You do not need to know what arrangement they have with their office. You just need to understand that the costs agents have are not the same. Their costs will affect what price they offer you if you decide to hire them and what services they provide you.

Huge Differences.

A relatively small percentage of agents sell the majority of homes each year. These agents know how to get the job done. The turnover rate in real estate is high. Most of the new agents will not be in the business at the end of two years.

Licensing requirements do not educate agents on how to sell a home. This comes from training and experience.

Service Options.

Like other industries you have many different types of service to choose from. There are agents and companies that offer to place your property on the Multiple Listing Service (MLS) for a flat fee of about $500 that is paid up front. When the home is sold the seller also pays the buyer's agent commission that is posted on the MLS. Two to Four percent for the buyer's agent, with three percent as the norm. The seller can usually decide the amount. We will talk later about the motivation the commission creates.

For a minimal flat fee the listing agent will post the homes information on the

MLS system and will help the seller with any offers that come in on the property. The seller will do all the other tasks the agent would normally do on a full service listing such as taking calls for showings and opening the home. Listing your home on the MLS for a flat fee may not be available in some areas.

Hiring an Agent to help you with all the details without going on the MLS is also an option. Use caution with this one, because the marketing the MLS provides is very valuable. It would make sense if you wanted help and you had a buyer line up. With this type of listing there is not a commission for a buyers agent and the home is not listed on the MLS and affiliated websites. The Agent markets the home other ways to find a buyer. The agent will provide services for you and look out for your best interests. You need to know when it is smart not to be on the MLS. Most of the time it is better to be on the MLS.

Usually the best option is full service on the MLS. The normal cost for full service or full representation ranges from four to seven percent of the sales price. Agents and brokers help the seller prepare and stage the home prior to listing the home. They provide the marketing for the home on the internet, and in print to find buyers for your home.

The agent helps you decide on your list price, provides safety and security information for showings. They usually supply a lockbox (keybox) for the property that allows other agents to access the home for showings. This also helps control who is allowed into the home as they have to be a part of the board of realtors to have access through the keybox. They also have a pin code for their device to get a key from the box so if someone found their device they would not be able to activate the box. Many keybox types also will not open during the night.

Agents take calls from buyers and agents to get buyers in your home and will work with them to get you an offer from a buyer.

When the offer comes in they review the offer with you and advise you of your different options and suggest solutions to problems in the offer and advise you in your negotiations. They help you understand the contract and other paperwork involved to sell your home. When an offer is accepted they help the seller meet the requirements of the contract. This includes disclosures from the seller to the buyer, title research, Covenants Conditions and Restrictions, deadlines for home inspections, appraisal, and special conditions of the offer.

They help find solutions to the challenges that come up prior to closing. At closing they work with the Title company (escrow company or attorney, if applicable) to prepare the closing documents and close the transaction.

Who you want.
Experience and attitude go a long way to get you what you want as a seller.

Real Estate Street Smarts

You want an agent with a good attitude who will look for solutions to any problems that come up, and is willing to ask his broker or other appropriate professionals when he or she does not have the answer; An agent that will explain the situation to you and educate you on possible options you have, and let **you** decide which way you want to handle the situations that come up.

A real estate agent or broker? All agents must have a broker who is responsible for them. An associate broker is a broker who is not responsible for the agents at their office. The principal broker is responsible for the other agents in their office. Experience of brokers vary. In Utah brokers have 120 additional hours of education, pass a state exam, and have the required experience points earned by each property they sell. They also must be a licensed agent for no less than three years. Many brokers have many more years of experience. Not all brokers help buyers and sellers some are managers only, some sell only, and some manage and sell.

Agents and brokers take continuing education and can earn designation showing additional education they have received. CRS (Certified Residential Specialist), GRI (Graduate Realtor Institute), and ABR (Accredited Buyer Representative). This training helps them serve you better. Qualifying to be a broker requires the largest time investment from the agent.

Realtor or a sales agent?

There is a difference between a Realtor and a sales agent. A Realtor is a member of the National Association of Realtors, and a member of a local association. They are also a member of the local Multiple Listing Service. Realtors are obligated to follow their code of ethics above and beyond the state regulations for licensees.

A sales agent is licensed with the state but is not part of the MLS or the code of ethics. Sales agents are most common in new construction working with builders that spend large amounts of money marketing their subdivisions.

For individual sellers and Some builders the advantages of a Realtor are best. The exposure from the MLS system is crucial. Take a look for yourself at **www.*realtor.com*** where you will find homes from all over the U.S. for sale. Your local MLS will have a public web site that automatically loads all the MLS listings for all to see.

On the MLS agents offer to pay the agent/broker who brings the buyer. In this way they all benefit by helping each other sell homes. This is a very effective system. Agents are watching the market for buyers with specific needs. Sometimes the home is sold in the first few days because a buyers agent has a search set up for their buyers needs. The system notifies them of your home as soon as it is listed.

The commission on the MLS motivates the agent to show and sell your home. When you are comparing listing agents, an important item to pay attention to is how much they are offering to the buyers agent on the MLS. If the total commission is six percent and they are offering two or two and a half percent to the buyers agent, they are putting you as the seller at a disadvantage.

Agents are motivated by earning money. If the commission is low there are agents that will not show the home. You can figure out what the norm is by checking to see what other homes are offering. You want the norm or higher. If your total commission, as the seller, is five percent ask them how much they will be offering the buyers agent. It is better for you as a seller if the listing agent discounts their own commission instead of the buyers agent's portion.

> ### FOOD FOR THOUGHT
>
> ## The Motivation You Want
> You want an Agent that will put your interest before their own.
>
> An Agent who will keep good communication with you.
>
> An Agent that will monitor the progress of your listing and move with the market when necessary.
>
> You want an Agent that will not just put your listing out to pasture.
>
> You want an Agent that will service and maintain the listing.

From your total of 5% this would mean the listing agent, the one the seller works with, would get two percent and the buyers agent would get three percent. This way, you don't miss out on any possible buyers for your home.

Agents should take the time to double check the listing information and check to make sure it pulls up on searches. They should check the links to see if they work correctly and are accurate.

Attention to detail affect your results as a seller. A simple typo can make your home invisible on the Internet. Certain changes can be made to your listing to make the home come up on autohotsheets that agents use to keep their active buyers informed on new listings and listing with changes that are within their search criteria.

Do your homework.
To find the right agent for your needs, take some time before you need to list your home to do a little research. Is there an agent that specializes in what you have?

Agents who have listings for sale and who have just sold homes in your area will know what people like about the area and will know which people the property appeals to. The agent will likely know the weaknesses of the area in comparison to other options available to buyers.

Having an agent that is available to show your home is important. This is not about how busy they are. It is more important that they answer their phone and return calls promptly. After all, buyers and agents can't see your home if they can not get a hold of your agent.

You do not need to select an agent blind. You can hand pick from the best agents and brokers available in your area. We can help you select agents based on their statistics. That way you will know you are getting an agent that will get the job done for you. You can pick agents based on sold price per foot, days on market, percentage of list price, or based on who is selling the most of what you have. More on our referral service later on.

What to look for in your first meeting.

What is the focus of the agent? Are they focused on what you want and need? In their discussion with you, do they make sure you understand, or are you left with unanswered questions?

Do they know your neighborhood? Do they have a good understanding of the current market conditions for your area? Do they show the knowledge and experience needed to prepare, stage, market, and negotiate the contract for your home.

Did they come on time to your appointment? In your meeting did they clearly explain the plan for marketing your home to secure a buyer? Did they educate you on your obligations on the listing contract and what you will be obligated to do on the purchase contract you will receive from a buyer? Or did they just say "sign here"?

When they went over the market data and pricing information, did they educate you on the market and let you decide how you want to price your home? When you asked for their recommendation on price did they ask you how quickly you need to sell? When they gave you a suggested price point did it make logical sense? If you look on the Internet at all the homes a buyer would look at does the price look appealing to a buyer?

You want the honest agent that will be completely upfront with you and blunt when necessary--the agent that will tell you that if you price your home above market value you will be priced too high and will not be attractive to buyers. A good agent will tell you to consider a higher price if you suggest a list price that is clearly too low. (You could do that to test them). They would explain to you that you would be pricing below market value and it would likely sell very fast at that price, but you may want to consider the highest possible price that would keep your home as the best value on the market or very close to the best value on the market.

In each situation ask yourself, "are they thinking of me and what is best for me or are they thinking of themselves". Sometimes the truth is not what the seller wants to hear. Do not punish an honest agent by hiring an agent that will tell you what you want to hear to get the listing.

Take the time to check the market data to verify what you have been told. Do not just hire the agent that gives you the highest price. The agent that would get you to price your home too high in order to get the listing, will benefit by having the work and the commission while wasting *your* time and money. The Honest agent risks not getting the work or the money in order to give you the truth!

An agent that would list your home well under value is concerned more about making a quick dollar for themselves than they are about making as much as possible for you.

Please check the market. After all, most buyers are just people looking for a home that works for them. They do not want to overpay, but you can guess they would love to underpay (get a deal).

What will the agent do to protect your family while the home is on the market. Did they bring up identity, property, and other theft risks? If you asked them about it do they have a plan for you? How are they protecting you as the seller from the buyer in the future? Do they understand the legal contracts and disclosures used to protect you now and in the future?

Problems will come up.

No matter who you pick do not expect your transaction to go perfectly. You should expect a few things to come up in the process. Think of it as part of the process. Having a great agent help you will allow you to avoid many of the problems that can come up. Their experience and knowledge will save you stress and money, however, it will not guarantee a transaction without problems. The experience and knowledge of your agent will help you know what to do when problems come up. You want an agent that will look out for your best interest when they suggest solutions.

Do you have a friend or family member that is an agent?

If you have a friend or family member that is not the right agent for the type of property you have, you still have an option that will work well for everyone. You will get the agent you really need, your friend will earn money for helping you find the right agent, and your specialized agent will earn money for getting the job done.

Your friend will make more per hour helping you this way than he would by completing the transaction for you. He will appreciate you for being so thoughtful.

A referral, here is how it works. In the U.S. Agents will share the commission by giving the agent (their brokerage actually) that referred a client to them a referral fee. This fee is negotiable. It depends on each agent on how much the referral fee would be. A common amount would be 25% of one side of the commission. It could be anything more or less. Some relocation companies will ask and get 40% from their referrals.

The referral fee applies only to one side of the transaction. This is usually 3% of sales price but it can be different, more or less. The reason this is great for everyone is simple. Your friend will not be required to spend all the time needed to get the job done. They will find the right agent and follow up with the agent and will receive 25% of the commission. This makes the time he spends helping you very profitable.

It is great for you because you will make more money on your property by having an agent that specializes in the type of property you are selling. The agent that sells your home is doing great because they get paid to do what they do best. It is a win, win for everyone.

If you do not have a friend or family member to help you find an agent, we want to help you. You can see our consulting and referral services on our web site at ***www.RESmartMoves.com***

With a referral you, as the seller, interview the chosen agents until you have the one that meets your needs. You stay in control, but have help finding agents that are well suited for your needs.

We can help you select a specialized agent anywhere in the U.S. for any type of property. And can also help you find an agent to assist and represent you on the buying side of a transaction. You end up with two people, who care about your transaction going well, for the price of one.

Real Estate Street Smarts

-Chapter 7-
Mortgage Basics, A Critical Piece Of Your Real Estate Puzzle.

Picking the right home loan is just as important as picking the right house. There are many loan products to choose from, so how do you know which one you need? The risks you take on and the affect it has on your personal finances are different depending on the type of loan you choose. It truly will be a great friend or possibly a terrible foe!

Let's start with the basics. Loans are part of a market, the financial market. At any given time the programs available to you, the requirements for the loan, and the cost to get the loan can change. These changes are based on the market. All loans are products that people are selling to you. They can change very quickly and drastically.

It is helpful to understand how it works. Like other markets, it is also supply and demand driven. When you go in and talk to a broker or a lender they give you a Good Faith Estimate of what is currently available to you as a borrower. This can change daily or even during the day. Loan programs are added or removed. Loan requirements get harder or easier. Interest rates go up or down.

Banks will sell the loans they make or they keep and service the loans. The reality for most is that the bank that gives the money to you takes your loan and puts it into a large bundle of loans they then sell to someone in the secondary lending market. The new lender will then service the loan until it is paid off or until they sell it to someone else.

Investors determine the supply of money available for home loans. As with any investment, investors look at the risk and reward. If the risk is high investors want a larger reward. If the investments are an unacceptable risk they will move their money into other things. They have many options, like stocks, bonds, treasury bills, real estate, venture capital, gold, oil, seeds etc.. To name only a few of their choices.

Investors look at the risk and reward to decide if they want to invest in the product. They look at the interest they will receive to help them make their choice. If inflation is high, they will want more interest for the loan. If they receive a return on their money equal to inflation, their money has not grown. If they earn less than inflation, it will not buy as much as before and is seen as a small loss.

If inflation is at 4% they break even on their money at 4%. So naturally when inflation is high the home loan rates are high. When inflation is low rates can be low. In the early 1980's 14% to 18% loans were your options. At this time CD's (Certificates of Deposit) and other investments also had higher rates of return to compensate for the high inflation.

63

Borrowers create the demand in the market. There is built-in demand because of the need for shelter and because most of us do not have cash to buy our homes. This level of demand is increased and decreased as loan products get more or less appealing to all of us as borrowers.

The mortgage interest rates below 5% have not been seen since the early 1960's. The current inflation is next to zero and the United States government has recently put approximately 1.2 trillion into the supply of funds to bring the rates lower and stimulate housing to help end the recession and bring economic recovery.

The Fed (centralized bank for the United States) controls the rate of interest they charge banks to borrow money. If banks can borrow funds at a low rate, they can also loan money to you at a low rate. They make a margin, meaning they charge you more interest than they are paying. The Fed rate is currently 0-.25%. It cannot go lower than this. They lower this rate to stimulate activity and growth in the economy. They also increase this base rate to slow down inflation. The increase of the rate makes the loans less affordable and increases the interest earnings of the money. This leads to less volume.

It is much like any other part of the economy. When things are slow you give incentives to get people interested in what you have. These investors are from inside and outside of the United States. Their motivation is the return or increase on their investment. If the risk is high they want higher interest rates in return.

These home loan bundles have been safe investments, until the recent credit crisis. The United States Government guarantee the loans held by Fannie Mae and Freddie Mac. Many investors put their money in the market with these companies because they saw it as a safe place to put their money. The United States Congress were pushing to get more people into home ownership which led to zero money down loans, varied loan programs such as interest only loans, and variable rate loans. This also provided easier lending requirements in some cases with lower credit scores required and no proof of income or ability to repay.

This would not be a risk the typical investor would make without the guarantee from the government that the money was safe. Investors want the borrower to have some of their own money in the deal that they could lose and they want better indicators of ability and willingness to pay back the money.

This problem was a small one when the prices of the homes securing the loans were going up quickly. If the borrower did not make the payment the bank could sell the home and get their money back. The crisis came when house values started falling. This brought large losses on these risky loans when they went bad.

There are many details that played a part in the crisis. The intent here is to just give you an idea of how things are interrelated and how they affect you. In our current situation, the home values are correcting, going down, to be in line once again with normal inflation and affordability for homeowners.

Many people who could get a home loan two years ago cannot qualify now, even if their situation is the same. This is due to the removal of many of the more risky loan programs.

Your options are much more restrictive now than they were in the boom of the 1990's through 2007. In our history we have come a very long way from requiring large down payments to the aggressive loan programs that allowed borrowers to finance 100% of the purchase price of the home plus the buyers closing costs and in some cases money for flooring or other updates. Cash out refinancing to buy a car, a boat, or consolidate debt gave many the artificial feeling and appearance of wealth. Investors and borrowers have changed with the economic changes to be more careful with debt.

Our current situation only feels restrictive because we remember how it was just a few years ago. What we need to remember is that the 3.5% down payment required by FHA (Federal Housing Administration) is only up .5% from what it was and the conventional requirement of 5-10% down is reasonable and will help stabilize the market. The down payment requirement will help keep foreclosures down and as a result keep the market prices more stable. We don't know if they will make the requirements more difficult or less difficult in the future.

Loan programs.
You need to know about the loan programs available to you. You need to understand their advantages and their risks. A few of the programs you need to know about are 30-year fixed loans, 15-year fixed, adjustable-rate mortgages, and interest-only mortgages.

A 30-year fixed home loan is a very popular home loan. Your monthly payment is calculated based on paying the interest you owe the lender and paying off the home loan to a balance of zero in 30 years. Your interest rate stays the same for the entire 30-year period. Fixed-rate loans come with a little higher interest rates than loans with interest rates that can change. They are less risky because the interest payment never changes, so you don't have to worry about current rates going way up and making your house payment unaffordable.

There is risk with any loan you take. The risk is that if you do not pay, the lender can take the house in order to get their money back. It is a legal process called foreclosure. So what you risk is the house, and all of the time and money you have put into it. If you don't make your payment, but you only owe 20% of the value of the home the bank will work to get their money from you. The bank would likely sell the home quickly for 60 to 80% of its market value. After they have their money including their late fees, attorney, and other fees they are required to give you the balance of the money left from the sale, if any. If you sell your home you would likely get 90 to 100% of its value, minus your closing costs. In the next chapter you will learn how to reduce this risk and how you can eliminate the risk altogether.

A 15-year fixed loan is similar to the 30-year fixed loan as both have fixed interest rates, but different because the payment required each month is higher on a 15-year loan. The 15-year loan is financially a better deal. The interest rate is lower, you pay off your home faster and the lender gets their money back faster. The reason a 15-year loan has more risk than a 30-year loan is the fact that the monthly payment is higher on a 15-year loan, so if you lost your job or became unable to earn new income you would go through your savings at a faster rate and could possibly put your home in jeopardy. These two loan types are the least risky. On both of these loan types the balance of the loan is getting smaller each month as you make payments.

Watch out for what we call balloon payments! You can have a loan that has a payment schedule based on the 30-year loan, but with a 15-year or any year amount balloon payment that would require you to pay off the balance of the loan at the time of the balloon. We had this one sprung on us at closing on the first home my wife and I purchased. This balloon payment increases your risk because the entire balance of the loan is due in fifteen years even though the payment is based on a thirty-year loan schedule. This leaves more than half the loan balance that must be paid off. If interest rates are up or you do not qualify for a loan at the time it becomes due, it can force you sell or lose your home.

There are variations of these programs that are fixed loans with interest buy-downs. Buy-downs are prepaid interest at closing to buy down the monthly payment for a fixed term, one year, two years, and in some cases the whole term of the loan.

To figure out if this would be smart financially on a full-term buy-down you can calculate the cost of the buy-down with the monthly savings to calculate how many months before you break-even, and then after that date you start to save money.

If your break-even point is in three years, and you keep the mortgage for longer than three years it is a better deal. But if you sell your home or refinance your home sooner than the three years it becomes more expensive. What you risk is some of your money.

With a temporary payment buy-down, like a 2-1 buy-down, you are only buying the rate down for a few years. In the case of the 2-1 buy-down your payment is lower for the first two years of the loan

---

FOOD FOR THOUGHT

It would take three years of saving 50 dollars a month to break-even on $1800 spent on a buy down.

because you expect pay increases in the years to come making the higher payment more affordable. The first year is the lowest; the next year is in between the first year's payment and the permanent payment after the second year until the end of the loan. The risk here is increased because although it is based on fixed interest rates, you do have an unknown in your future. The pay increases you thought you would get might not come. You can put your house at risk because of the inability to pay the increased amounts in year two, or after year three.

You also need to consider with any buy-down if you can afford the upfront cost of the buy-down. After all, you could take that money and have it in your savings account to make your loan payments if needed.

Another loan type is adjustable-rate mortgages (ARM); they come in many types and variations. The main difference and reason for the increased risk to you is the unknown future. The interest rate on an adjustable rate mortgage moves with the market. They are based off of the prime rate set by the FED or an index, like the LIBOR index, London Inter-Bank Offered Rate. The LIBOR index is based on the average interest rate five major international banks charge at a given moment. If the index or prime rate is 4% and your loan is prime plus 2% your payment will be calculated on 6%. If prime moves to 6% you pay 8%. If you remember the interest rate chart showing how high the interest rates can get you can see that your payment can change significantly with the market changes. Most of these programs will allow up to a 2 point (2 %) increase per year. You have to read your specific program to know how it works, as they can vary.

Your interest rate is a little lower on these programs than the current available fixed-loan programs. With these loan programs you risk the rates increasing and the possibility of having your monthly payment no longer being manageable.

These loans have many variations, such as loans that are fixed interest rate and fixed monthly payment for 5 years then they change to a variable-rate for the rest of the term of the loan. Or three year fixed then variable-rate to give you an idea. With these modifications your risk is not knowing for sure what will happen in the years to come. The borrowers most likely to use these programs are the ones who know they will be refinancing or selling before the loan becomes a variable-rate. A word of caution is the fact that life does not always go as planned so even though you don't plan on having your loan longer than the fixed period your plans can change. This is why this loan program is more risky than a fixed-rate loan, but a little less risky than a pure adjustable rate loan. Adjustable-rate loans are also paid down each month until they are paid off. This makes them less risky than interest only loans.

Interest-only loans are just that, a lower monthly payment because you are not lowering the balance of the loan each month. You are not ever paying off your loan. These loans can be fixed for a number of years, then change to adjustable, or they can be adjustable for the entire term of the loan. In any case these are the most risky loan options available.

The lowest monthly payment available draws borrowers in but the risk they take is not worth the lower payment. You would be better off financially to buy a more affordable home that you are likely to still own five to ten years down the road. The availability of these loans are now very limited as the risk is also high for the investors.

Getting the loan you want.

The rate for your loan and your ability to get the loan will be based on your credit score, your down payment, and your ability to repay the loan. If you do not have 20% down you will be required to pay for mortgage insurance. It is a monthly premium to insure the bank against losses that arise from the borrowers failure to repay the loan. If you have equity, or a down payment, of 20% or more you are not required to have the insurance, because the loan is not a high risk. This is because you have more to lose if you don't pay and the bank is less likely to take a large loss if they have to take the home and sell it.

Your monthly payment almost always includes an escrow payment for property taxes and fire insurance. If your home is located in an area with other known risks like flood zones you may be required to buy other insurance products for the property. Banks require this money to be paid by you monthly, held by them until the bill is due to make sure the property is current on taxes and has the required insurance coverage. The banks don't want the risk of loss if there was a problem with tax or insurance items.

If your home burns down they don't want to lose the value of the asset securing their loan to you. Banks make sure you pay your property tax because a government lien is always first priority and is first to get paid no matter what date liens were filed. So if you don't pay your $2,000 tax bill the bank could lose their first lien holder position on the title of the property. That risk is the same reason a second mortgage is always more expensive than a first mortgage. Their risk of loss is much higher.

You may also have a Home Owners Association that requires a monthly payment. This is also added to your monthly costs that lenders consider as they look at your finances to determine if you can afford the loan you are applying for.

Lenders have what is called debt-to-income ratio's they use to calculate your ability to repay the loan. There are two types, front-end ratios and back-end ratios. The front-end is your gross income compared to your home loan payment in the form of a percentage of income.

The back-end is your gross income compared to your home loan payment and all other debt payments. They have rules on what is acceptable or not, and this can change as banks change their programs.

When you go into a lender and get an estimate from them they get all your financial info; what money you have coming in, what money you have saved, what you own that has value, and what your expenses are. They then plug in the front-end and back-end ratio's to give you a loan amount that you are pre-approved for.

Lenders differ on this, as some will give you an amount that is as high as they think they can possibly get a loan for. Other lenders will give you an amount that is lower than the edge to help you avoid potential problems qualifying for the loan. Some lenders may even just ask you what amount you are thinking to borrow to see if it is acceptable for the loan programs they offer.

Pushing this amount as high as you can is not a good idea. It causes problems as it makes the approval questionable when you are committed on a purchase contract. All it takes is a little change in your finances to put you above acceptable limits. Remember your income has to meet the terms of the program. How long you have been at your current job, in the same industry, or if you are on salary or commission affect how the lender sees you as a risk.

There is incredible wisdom in following the wise council to spend what will be very comfortable and what will allow

> ### FOOD FOR THOUGHT
>
> **Financial planners will tell you to spend 25 % ideally, 25-35% if necessary, of your gross income on your housing. Lenders will lend you much more than these levels. What they are willing to lend and what you should spend are usually two completely different things.**

funds for the many other things that come up in life. In my state of Utah many borrowers pay 10% or more of their income to their Church for charity and other programs. Lenders do not factor these costs in when they calculate your debt to income ratios.

Carefully plan your budget, as this one thing will reduce the risk of loss with your home loan.

There are different loan products available to you. If you have served in the United Sates Military you may qualify for a VA (Veterans Administration) loan. These loans have lower down payment requirements as well as less strict approval requirements, and lower interest rates. Check out *www.homeloans.va.gov* to see who can get a VA loan.

FHA loans are U.S. government insured loans. These loans have less borrower requirements than a conventional loan and a lower down payment requirement of 3.5%. You can only have one FHA loan at a time and you must live in the home, at the time you get your financing, for one year. The home must meet the guidelines for the loan, which is more restrictive than a conventional loan. With these loans you pay an upfront mortgage insurance fee of which a portion can become refundable if the loan is paid off early. The interest rate can be a little lower than a conventional loan. FHA and VA loans have loan amount limits that are set based on the median home prices in the area. These price limits are higher for conventional loans. Conventional loans are loans not insured by FHA or VA.

Conforming loans are loans that meet all the requirements to be sold to Fannie Mae and Freddie Mac. The interest rates are slightly higher than FHA but the mortgage insurance, if applicable, is only monthly with no upfront mortgage insurance. The minimum down payment requirement is 5-10% for owner-occupied loans. 5% for first time homebuyers.

The costs and rules are different for financing rentals/investment properties. There is more risk because investors do not live in the property. Investor's pay more money down and a higher interest rate. Currently you can expect one percent higher on your interest rate and twenty to twenty five percent required as a down payment. Investors who have a landlord history of one year or more can count 75% of the rent as income to qualify for the loan.

Second homes and vacation home loans are available at increased cost because of the added risk to the lender and the borrower must qualify for both their homes. If you want two homes I recommend paying cash for your second home.

Non-conforming loans currently are becoming less popular, more expensive, and less available. They are for those borrowers who do not meet the conforming requirements. They come with higher costs, as they are also higher risk. It may be the only option for some credit scores and types of income. Also, how long you have been at your current job, and how long you have been self-employed can put you in this category even if you have a great credit score.

Jumbo loans are high dollar loans above the conventional, conforming loan limits. They are more risky for the lender so lenders require higher down payments and higher interest rates for these loans.

Most, if not all of these loan programs will allow the seller to pay your closing costs for you, meaning it allows you to finance the closing costs into your loan.

Items you will be paying for in your closing cost include a title insurance premium for the lender for insurance coverage in the amount of the loan, title fees to prepare, settle, record and close the transaction, prorated taxes, prorated insurance, mortgage insurance, HOA transfer fees possibly, loan origination fees, appraisal fee, inspection fees, and other loan processing fees. These are one-time fees paid at closing.

Real Estate Street Smarts

When you close on your home loan you are given a settlement statement and closing documents that show these costs. You will be required to approve these costs and terms of the loan with your signature. Take the time to double-check what you are getting. If changes are made and you sign you are committed to the changes. Though there are many documents required for financing your home it is smart to read and discuss what you sign.

Pay off your loan early! Make sure your loan does not have a pre-payment penalty. You can also check with your lender to see if they allow bi-monthly payments. This will save you a lot of money on interest over the life of the loan. You pay one month ahead and twice a month stopping the interest from accruing more often and, in affect, saving you money. Lenders are getting smarter about this and have started to only apply your payment when it is the complete amount.

You can also significantly decrease the time it takes to pay off your home by paying more principle as you go. Make an extra payment each year or just add a hundred dollars or so each month. Look at how much you can save on interest.

When you buy your home, you pay the interest on the loan at closing so you end up skipping a housing payment for one month. But if you make the payment anyway, you will pay your loan off one year sooner since the entire payment goes to pay down your loan balance.

REGULAR PAYMENT SCHEDULE

YEAR	TOTAL PAYMENT 1199.1	INTEREST 6%	PRINCIPAL	BALANCE 200,000
1	14,389	11,933	2,456	197,544
2	14,389	11,782	2,607	194,937
3 TO 5	43,168	34,340	8,828	186,109
6 TO 10	71,946	53,209	18,737	167,372
11 TO 20	143,892	84,528	59,364	108,008
21 TO 24.6	65,950	24,347	41,604	66,404
24.6 TO 30	77,943	11,539	66,404	-
TOTALS	**431,677**	**231,677**	**200,000**	**ZERO**

ADDITIONAL ANNUAL PRINCIPAL PAYMENT
($100 EXTRA PER MONTH)

YEAR	TOTAL PAYMENT	INTEREST	PRINCIPAL	BALANCE
	1299.1	**6%**		**200,000**
1	15,589	11,900	3,690	196,310
2	15,589	11,672	3,917	192,393
3 TO 5	46,768	33,506	13,262	179,132
6 TO 10	77,946	49,798	28,148	150,984
11 TO 20	155,892	66,712	89,180	61,804
21 TO 24.6	70,754	8,951	61,804	-
TOTALS	**382,538**	**182,538**	**200,000**	**ZERO**
SAVINGS	**$49,139**			

YOU CUT MORE THAN 5 YEARS OFF YOUR LOAN AND SAVE $49,139 BY PAYING $100 MORE PER MONTH!

Take a look at this full amortization schedule to see how the loans work. You will notice at first the amount you are paying down is small but it gets much larger toward the end of the loan. At first paying extra has the affect of paying one and a half months down instead of only one.

30 YEAR PAYMENT SCHEDULE

PMT #	TOTAL PAYMENT	INTEREST	PRINCIPAL	BALANCE
		6%		**200,000**
1	1199.1	1,000	199	199,801
2	1199.1	999	200	199,601
3	1199.1	998	201	199,400
4	1199.1	997	202	199,198
5	1199.1	996	203	198,994
6	1199.1	995	204	198,790
7	1199.1	994	205	198,585
8	1199.1	993	206	198,379
9	1199.1	992	207	198,172
10	1199.1	991	208	197,964
11	1199.1	990	209	197,754
12	1199.1	989	210	197,544
13	1199.1	988	211	197,333
14	1199.1	987	212	197,120
15	1199.1	986	213	196,907

Real Estate Street Smarts

PMT #	PAYMENT	INTEREST	PRINCIPAL	BALANCE
16	1199.1	985	215	196,692
17	1199.1	983	216	196,476
18	1199.1	982	217	196,260
19	1199.1	981	218	196,042
20	1199.1	980	219	195,823
21	1199.1	979	220	195,603
22	1199.1	978	221	195,382
23	1199.1	977	222	195,160
24	1199.1	976	223	194,936
25	1199.1	975	224	194,712
26	1199.1	974	226	194,487
27	1199.1	972	227	194,260
28	1199.1	971	228	194,032
29	1199.1	970	229	193,803
30	1199.1	969	230	193,573
31	1199.1	968	231	193,342
32	1199.1	967	232	193,109
33	1199.1	966	234	192,876
34	1199.1	964	235	192,641
35	1199.1	963	236	192,405
36	1199.1	962	237	192,168
37	1199.1	961	238	191,930
38	1199.1	960	239	191,690
39	1199.1	958	241	191,450
40	1199.1	957	242	191,208
41	1199.1	956	243	190,965
42	1199.1	955	244	190,721
43	1199.1	954	245	190,475
44	1199.1	952	247	190,228
45	1199.1	951	248	189,980
46	1199.1	950	249	189,731
47	1199.1	949	250	189,481
48	1199.1	947	252	189,229
49	1199.1	946	253	188,976
50	1199.1	945	254	188,722
51	1199.1	944	255	188,466
52	1199.1	942	257	188,210
53	1199.1	941	258	187,952
54	1199.1	940	259	187,692
55	1199.1	938	261	187,432
56	1199.1	937	262	187,170
57	1199.1	936	263	186,906
58	1199.1	935	265	186,642
59	1199.1	933	266	186,376
60	1199.1	932	267	186,109
61	1199.1	931	269	185,840
62	1199.1	929	270	185,570

Real Estate Street Smarts

PMT #	PAYMENT	INTEREST	PRINCIPAL	BALANCE
63	1199.1	928	271	185,299
64	1199.1	926	273	185,026
65	1199.1	925	274	184,753
66	1199.1	924	275	184,477
67	1199.1	922	277	184,200
68	1199.1	921	278	183,922
69	1199.1	920	279	183,643
70	1199.1	918	281	183,362
71	1199.1	917	282	183,080
72	1199.1	915	284	182,796
73	1199.1	914	285	182,511
74	1199.1	913	287	182,224
75	1199.1	911	288	181,936
76	1199.1	910	289	181,647
77	1199.1	908	291	181,356
78	1199.1	907	292	181,064
79	1199.1	905	294	180,770
80	1199.1	904	295	180,475
81	1199.1	902	297	180,178
82	1199.1	901	298	179,880
83	1199.1	899	300	179,580
84	1199.1	898	301	179,279
85	1199.1	896	303	178,976
86	1199.1	895	304	178,672
87	1199.1	893	306	178,366
88	1199.1	892	307	178,059
89	1199.1	890	309	177,750
90	1199.1	889	310	177,440
91	1199.1	887	312	177,128
92	1199.1	886	313	176,814
93	1199.1	884	315	176,499
94	1199.1	882	317	176,183
95	1199.1	881	318	175,865
96	1199.1	879	320	175,545
97	1199.1	878	321	175,223
98	1199.1	876	323	174,900
99	1199.1	875	325	174,576
100	1199.1	873	326	174,250
101	1199.1	871	328	173,922
102	1199.1	870	329	173,592
103	1199.1	868	331	173,261
104	1199.1	866	333	172,928
105	1199.1	865	334	172,594
106	1199.1	863	336	172,258
107	1199.1	861	338	171,920
108	1199.1	860	340	171,580
109	1199.1	858	341	171,239
110	1199.1	856	343	170,896

Real Estate Street Smarts

PMT #	PAYMENT	INTEREST	PRINCIPAL	BALANCE
111	1199.1	854	345	170,552
112	1199.1	853	346	170,205
113	1199.1	851	348	169,857
114	1199.1	849	350	169,508
115	1199.1	848	352	169,156
116	1199.1	846	353	168,803
117	1199.1	844	355	168,448
118	1199.1	842	357	168,091
119	1199.1	840	359	167,732
120	1199.1	839	360	167,372
121	1199.1	837	362	167,009
122	1199.1	835	364	166,645
123	1199.1	833	366	166,279
124	1199.1	831	368	165,912
125	1199.1	830	370	165,542
126	1199.1	828	371	165,171
127	1199.1	826	373	164,798
128	1199.1	824	375	164,422
129	1199.1	822	377	164,045
130	1199.1	820	379	163,667
131	1199.1	818	381	163,286
132	1199.1	816	383	162,903
133	1199.1	815	385	162,519
134	1199.1	813	387	162,132
135	1199.1	811	388	161,744
136	1199.1	809	390	161,353
137	1199.1	807	392	160,961
138	1199.1	805	394	160,567
139	1199.1	803	396	160,170
140	1199.1	801	398	159,772
141	1199.1	799	400	159,372
142	1199.1	797	402	158,970
143	1199.1	795	404	158,565
144	1199.1	793	406	158,159
145	1199.1	791	408	157,751
146	1199.1	789	410	157,340
147	1199.1	787	412	156,928
148	1199.1	785	414	156,514
149	1199.1	783	417	156,097
150	1199.1	780	419	155,678
151	1199.1	778	421	155,258
152	1199.1	776	423	154,835
153	1199.1	774	425	154,410
154	1199.1	772	427	153,983
155	1199.1	770	429	153,554
156	1199.1	768	431	153,122
157	1199.1	766	433	152,689

Real Estate Street Smarts

PMT #	PAYMENT	INTEREST	PRINCIPAL	BALANCE
158	1199.1	763	436	152,253
159	1199.1	761	438	151,815
160	1199.1	759	440	151,375
161	1199.1	757	442	150,933
162	1199.1	755	444	150,489
163	1199.1	752	447	150,042
164	1199.1	750	449	149,593
165	1199.1	748	451	149,142
166	1199.1	746	453	148,689
167	1199.1	743	456	148,233
168	1199.1	741	458	147,775
169	1199.1	739	460	147,315
170	1199.1	737	463	146,852
171	1199.1	734	465	146,388
172	1199.1	732	467	145,920
173	1199.1	730	469	145,451
174	1199.1	727	472	144,979
175	1199.1	725	474	144,505
176	1199.1	723	477	144,028
177	1199.1	720	479	143,549
178	1199.1	718	481	143,068
179	1199.1	715	484	142,584
180	1199.1	713	486	142,098
181	1199.1	710	489	141,609
182	1199.1	708	491	141,118
183	1199.1	706	494	140,625
184	1199.1	703	496	140,129
185	1199.1	701	498	139,630
186	1199.1	698	501	139,129
187	1199.1	696	503	138,626
188	1199.1	693	506	138,120
189	1199.1	691	508	137,612
190	1199.1	688	511	137,100
191	1199.1	686	514	136,587
192	1199.1	683	516	136,071
193	1199.1	680	519	135,552
194	1199.1	678	521	135,031
195	1199.1	675	524	134,507
196	1199.1	673	527	133,980
197	1199.1	670	529	133,451
198	1199.1	667	532	132,919
199	1199.1	665	535	132,385
200	1199.1	662	537	131,847
201	1199.1	659	540	131,308
202	1199.1	657	543	130,765
203	1199.1	654	545	130,220
204	1199.1	651	548	129,672

Real Estate Street Smarts

PMT #	PAYMENT	INTEREST	PRINCIPAL	BALANCE
205	1199.1	648	551	129,121
206	1199.1	646	553	128,567
207	1199.1	643	556	128,011
208	1199.1	640	559	127,452
209	1199.1	637	562	126,890
210	1199.1	634	565	126,326
211	1199.1	632	567	125,758
212	1199.1	629	570	125,188
213	1199.1	626	573	124,615
214	1199.1	623	576	124,039
215	1199.1	620	579	123,460
216	1199.1	617	582	122,878
217	1199.1	614	585	122,293
218	1199.1	611	588	121,706
219	1199.1	609	591	121,115
220	1199.1	606	594	120,522
221	1199.1	603	596	119,925
222	1199.1	600	599	119,326
223	1199.1	597	602	118,723
224	1199.1	594	605	118,118
225	1199.1	591	609	117,509
226	1199.1	588	612	116,898
227	1199.1	584	615	116,283
228	1199.1	581	618	115,665
229	1199.1	578	621	115,044
230	1199.1	575	624	114,421
231	1199.1	572	627	113,794
232	1199.1	569	630	113,163
233	1199.1	566	633	112,530
234	1199.1	563	636	111,894
235	1199.1	559	640	111,254
236	1199.1	556	643	110,611
237	1199.1	553	646	109,965
238	1199.1	550	649	109,316
239	1199.1	547	653	108,663
240	1199.1	543	656	108,008
241	1199.1	540	659	107,349
242	1199.1	537	662	106,686
243	1199.1	533	666	106,021
244	1199.1	530	669	105,352
245	1199.1	527	672	104,679
246	1199.1	523	676	104,004
247	1199.1	520	679	103,324
248	1199.1	517	682	102,642
249	1199.1	513	686	101,956
250	1199.1	510	689	101,267
251	1199.1	506	693	100,574
252	1199.1	503	696	99,878

Real Estate Street Smarts

PMT #	PAYMENT	INTEREST	PRINCIPAL	BALANCE
253	1199.1	499	700	99,178
254	1199.1	496	703	98,475
255	1199.1	492	707	97,768
256	1199.1	489	710	97,058
257	1199.1	485	714	96,344
258	1199.1	482	717	95,627
259	1199.1	478	721	94,906
260	1199.1	475	725	94,181
261	1199.1	471	728	93,453
262	1199.1	467	732	92,721
263	1199.1	464	735	91,986
264	1199.1	460	739	91,246
265	1199.1	456	743	90,504
266	1199.1	453	747	89,757
267	1199.1	449	750	89,007
268	1199.1	445	754	88,253
269	1199.1	441	758	87,495
270	1199.1	437	762	86,733
271	1199.1	434	765	85,968
272	1199.1	430	769	85,198
273	1199.1	426	773	84,425
274	1199.1	422	777	83,648
275	1199.1	418	781	82,867
276	1199.1	414	785	82,083
277	1199.1	410	789	81,294
278	1199.1	406	793	80,501
279	1199.1	403	797	79,705
280	1199.1	399	801	78,904
281	1199.1	395	805	78,100
282	1199.1	390	809	77,291
283	1199.1	386	813	76,478
284	1199.1	382	817	75,662
285	1199.1	378	821	74,841
286	1199.1	374	825	74,016
287	1199.1	370	829	73,187
288	1199.1	366	833	72,354
289	1199.1	362	837	71,517
290	1199.1	358	842	70,675
291	1199.1	353	846	69,829
292	1199.1	349	850	68,979
293	1199.1	345	854	68,125
294	1199.1	341	858	67,267
295	1199.1	336	863	66,404
296	1199.1	332	867	65,537
297	1199.1	328	871	64,665
298	1199.1	323	876	63,790
299	1199.1	319	880	62,909
300	1199.1	315	885	62,025

Real Estate Street Smarts

PMT #	PAYMENT	INTEREST	PRINCIPAL	BALANCE
301	1199.1	310	889	61,136
302	1199.1	306	893	60,243
303	1199.1	301	898	59,345
304	1199.1	297	902	58,442
305	1199.1	292	907	57,535
306	1199.1	288	911	56,624
307	1199.1	283	916	55,708
308	1199.1	279	921	54,787
309	1199.1	274	925	53,862
310	1199.1	269	930	52,932
311	1199.1	265	934	51,998
312	1199.1	260	939	51,059
313	1199.1	255	944	50,115
314	1199.1	251	949	49,167
315	1199.1	246	953	48,213
316	1199.1	241	958	47,255
317	1199.1	236	963	46,292
318	1199.1	231	968	45,325
319	1199.1	227	972	44,352
320	1199.1	222	977	43,375
321	1199.1	217	982	42,393
322	1199.1	212	987	41,406
323	1199.1	207	992	40,414
324	1199.1	202	997	39,417
325	1199.1	197	1,002	38,414
326	1199.1	192	1,007	37,407
327	1199.1	187	1,012	36,395
328	1199.1	182	1,017	35,378
329	1199.1	177	1,022	34,356
330	1199.1	172	1,027	33,329
331	1199.1	167	1,032	32,296
332	1199.1	161	1,038	31,259
333	1199.1	156	1,043	30,216
334	1199.1	151	1,048	29,168
335	1199.1	146	1,053	28,115
336	1199.1	141	1,059	27,056
337	1199.1	135	1,064	25,992
338	1199.1	130	1,069	24,923
339	1199.1	125	1,074	23,849
340	1199.1	119	1,080	22,769
341	1199.1	114	1,085	21,684
342	1199.1	108	1,091	20,593
343	1199.1	103	1,096	19,497
344	1199.1	97	1,102	18,395
345	1199.1	92	1,107	17,288
346	1199.1	86	1,113	16,175
347	1199.1	81	1,118	15,057

PMT #	PAYMENT	INTEREST	PRINCIPAL	BALANCE
348	1199.1	75	1,124	13,933
349	1199.1	70	1,129	12,804
350	1199.1	64	1,135	11,669
351	1199.1	58	1,141	10,528
352	1199.1	53	1,146	9,382
353	1199.1	47	1,152	8,229
354	1199.1	41	1,158	7,071
355	1199.1	35	1,164	5,908
356	1199.1	30	1,170	4,738
357	1199.1	24	1,175	3,563
358	1199.1	18	1,181	2,381
359	1199.1	12	1,187	1,194
360	1200.1	6	1,194	0

TOTALS

	431,677	231,677	200,000	ZERO

*On a $200,000 home you will have spent **$431,677 in 30 years**.*
*The value of the home after 30 years will likely be **$800,000***

If you want huge savings consider a fifteen-year loan.

15 YEAR REGULAR PAYMENT SCHEDULE

YEAR	PMT#	PAYMENT	6% INT	PRINCIPAL	BALANCE
					200,000
1	1	1687.71	1,000	688	199,312
5	60	1687.71	765	923	152,018
10	120	1687.71	443	1,245	87,299
15	179	1687.71	17	1,671	1,680
FINAL	180	1688.71	8	1,680	0

15 YEAR TOTALS	**303,789**	**103,789**	**200,000**	
30 YEAR TOTALS	431,677	231,677	200,000	

SAVINGS $127,888
YOU SAVE $127,888 ON INTEREST AND PAY OFF YOUR HOME IN 15 YEARS!

What a great system of opportunity! We should all be very grateful for investors who loan out their money to people like us, making it possible for each of us to own a home years before we could save the money to buy a home on our own. For some, saving money in amounts so large would not ever happen.

We should not despise a company or a person who is willing to let us use their money to allow us to accomplish our own goals and dreams. The interest we pay is usually much less than the increase in housing costs. We pay approximately two and a half times the amount we borrow over a thirty-year loan period, but the home will likely be worth four times what we paid for it after thirty years and we will have enjoyed the property all the while. If we had been saving for thirty years to buy, we would have also had rent expenses that would have increased over the years.

Home loans are truly good for the investor and for us as borrowers. What makes a home loan different from a car loan, motor home, couch, or mobile home loan is the increase in real property's (land) value over the long term. This is why financial planners will tell you that buying expensive personal property items like these with a loan is a very bad and expensive choice financially.

Prepare yourself to give this same gift to someone else by saving your money so that you can be the investor and earn interest while helping someone else live his or her dream.

Real Estate Street Smarts

-Chapter 8-
Prepare To Buy A Home.

It is not just your house it is your home. You can't expect something this great without work and sacrifice. Smart people prepare for their future by building on a solid foundation. Buying a home before you are ready is much like building a stick house on the sand. It is temporary and eventually comes to nothing when there is bad weather.

Before you jump in your car and start looking at homes, you need a set of plans to help you achieve your goals for long-term security and success.   Plans don't help if you do not follow them in detail. If you build without plans you gamble all your efforts. You risk all you have done, with the potential of losing everything just to get started sooner.

I can tell you from experience that planning will make the difference between success and failure. When you fail, you will plan better the next time, but the school of hard knocks is expensive, so save yourself the time and money and do it right the first time. You should be proud that you're building strong. This is a distance race, not a sprint. You have to finish to win.

You win by starting with your finances. To have a stable and secure foundation to build on and to limit your risk of loss you need to dig deep. You cannot start building your visible (above ground) future until you solidify the footings and foundation that will hold your home and your personal finances.

> ### FOOD FOR THOUGHT
>
> **No matter your income, you need to have a budget and you need to save money for your future. Your savings and your ability to live within your monthly budget provide you a strong foundation to build the home of your future.**

You will need to rent while you save. You will need to decide what you should spend on rent while you save the money needed to purchase a home of your own. The less you spend on rent the more you can save for your future.

There are many great places to get information on budgeting, you can find information online and at the library. I personally like the material from my church for basics on budgeting and financing. It teaches us to avoid debt and live well within our means.

For free money management information go to *www.providentliving.org* or go to *www.lds.org* then input the words "money management" in the search field in the upper right. You will find many resources listed to help you, including a talk from 1975 that has been used as a money management pamphlet called <u>One For The Money</u> by Elder Marvin J. Ashton. It is very good as are the many other materials on the subject.

I will give you a very basic idea of what you need to accomplish with your budget.

You should have a written budget for every month. You should plan how you are going to use the money you receive each month. If you don't have a place for your money it will find a place for itself. It will end up as things that don't get you where you want to be.

Your budget should include all your mandatory expenses. Food, heat, shelter, clothing, utilities, insurance, car payment (if you have one), gas, supplies, miscellaneous (like oil changes and repairs) and so on. You need to remember to save 10 to 15% of your income. This will first go to your rainy day savings, and then when your savings are in order it will go to different specific investments for your future, such as a down payment for a home.

If your expenses are too high and/or your income is too low you need to make changes. You either increase your income or you decrease your expenses/lifestyle or both. This may mean you need to sell a car, live in a different place or eat at home instead of eating out.

You cannot spend more than you make. This will lead to your financial collapse. Controlling your spending is more important than how much money you make. You can make a lot of money and be completely broke and you can also make little and be very wealthy. Work hard to make a good living, spend wisely and build wealth and security. Do not try to look wealthy, be wealthy! Wealth and security come from saving and making smart investments that increase your savings.

Everything you buy with borrowed money will cost you more. Your money will buy more when you pay cash. You are smart when you avoid paying interest charges especially on items that decline in value over time.

Look at how much extra you pay when you borrow and how much extra money you earn when you save and invest wisely.

Real Estate Street Smarts

CONSUMER LOAN AMORTIZATION

PAYMENT #	AMOUNT	INTEREST 8%	PRINCIPAL	BALANCE $15,000
1	304.15	100	204	14,796
13	304.15	83	221	12,237
25	304.15	65	239	9,466
37	304.15	45	259	6,465
49	304.15	23	281	3,215
60	304.15	2	302	(0)
TOTAL	**18,249**	**3,249**	**15,000**	

You spend $3,249 to buy an item now instead of saving and paying cash.
Interest can work for you when you save!

INVESTED AMOUNT   **$10,000**
AVERAGE RATE OF RETURN   **3%**
Compounded Annually

YEAR	INTEREST	BALANCE
1	300	10,300
2	309	10,609
3	318	10,927
4	328	11,255
5	338	11,593
6	348	11,941
7	358	12,299
8	369	12,668
9	380	13,048
10	391	13,439
11	403	13,842
12	415	14,258
13	428	14,685
14	441	15,126
15	454	15,580
16	467	16,047
17	481	16,528
18	496	17,024
19	511	17,535

Real Estate Street Smarts

YEAR	INTEREST	BALANCE
20	526	18,061
21	542	18,603
22	558	19,161
23	575	19,736
24	592	20,328
25	610	20,938
26	628	21,566
27	647	22,213
28	666	22,879
29	686	23,566
30	707	24,273
31	728	25,001
32	750	25,751
33	773	26,523
34	796	27,319
35	820	28,139

INVESTED AMOUNT   **$ 10,000**
AVERAGE 'RATE OF RETURN   **8%**
Compounded Annually

YEAR	INTEREST	BALANCE
1	800	10,800
2	864	11,664
3	933	12,597
4	1,008	13,605
5	1,088	14,693
6	1,175	15,869
7	1,269	17,138
8	1,371	18,509
9	1,481	19,990
10	1,599	21,589
11	1,727	23,316
12	1,865	25,182
13	2,015	27,196
14	2,176	29,372
15	2,350	31,722

FOOD FOR THOUGHT

The people who understand interest earn it.

The people Who don't pay it!

Real Estate Street Smarts

YEAR	INTEREST	BALANCE
16	2,538	34,259
17	2,741	37,000
18	2,960	39,960
19	3,197	43,157
20	3,453	46,610
21	3,729	50,338
22	4,027	54,365
23	4,349	58,715
24	4,697	63,412
25	5,073	68,485
26	5,479	73,964
27	5,917	79,881
28	6,390	86,271
29	6,902	93,173
30	7,454	100,627
31	8,050	108,677
32	8,694	117,371
33	9,390	126,760
34	10,141	136,901
35	10,952	147,853

Over the years your money makes a ton of money for you! At 8% interest and with leaving the earnings in to grow by the end of five years ten thousand dollars increases to fourteen thousand six hundred and ninety three dollars. That is 46% more than you started with. After thirty years it builds to over one hundred thousand dollars. **The people who understand interest earn it. The people who don't pay it!**

You need to have three to six months of your living expenses in savings if you are an employee with what you feel is a secure job. If you own your own business you need to save nine to twelve months worth of living expenses, and if you work for a company that has frequent layoffs, consider saving as much as a self-employed person.

This emergency fund will reduce your risk of loss or damages if you lose your job, have decreased earnings, or have a serious incident that reduces your income. It gives you time to fix the problem, what ever it may be. It gives you confidence in yourself, and your family's future. It also makes it possible for you to avoid financing charges when unexpected events happen, like a car repair or an accident.

When you have your savings in place you can pay for the emergency item, then build up your savings again in the following months with money from your investment budget. You will avoid interest charges and you will be making a little interest on your money if you have it in a money market or savings account. After your savings is back to where it should be, you start adding to investment funds again.

After you have your emergency savings in place you need to start saving your budgeted amount of 10 to 15 % to build a fund for your down payment and closing costs to buy a house. This will likely come before other investments but does not have to. Depending on how you structure the purchase, you will need anywhere from 3.5 to 8% or more in cash to get into your home.

There are home inspections and test that are paid for before you get your home loan and close on your home. You have earnest money (usually less than 1% of purchase price) that you give at the time you make the offer to the seller to show you are serious about purchasing their home. It is counted at closing, as part of your down payment, but is required up front.

Another thing to think about is the money you will need to furnish, decorate, update, paint, or clean the home. Don't forget moving expenses, cost for deposits to set up utilities etc.. Each item may not be much by themselves but they do add up so plan ahead.

You don't need new or nice things for your first home. If you are fortunate you may have much of what you need already or have friends and family that have things you can use until you get your own.

I think you will be surprised how incredible it can be to sit on a hand me down couch or a cheap bean bag in the home you now own! It is all about perspective and the fact that you know where you are headed. You are building strong, and you are building smart. Many nice things will come later. If they come too soon they will just hold you back.

When you have all these funds saved you will have your finances ready. As you research and figure out loan options that work with your budget you will start to see a dream becoming a reality.

Don't worry if it takes a long time. It is a lot faster to build strong in the first place instead of building quickly, having it fall apart and having to start over years later. You will be far ahead if you follow the plan to do it right the first time.

Real Estate Street Smarts

-Chapter 9-
With So Many Property Types, Which One Is Right For You?

Now that you are ready to buy, what should you buy? There are many types of real estate. Buying the right style and type of home with the features that fit your lifestyle will increase your enjoyment of the property and will make you more likely to live in the home longer. This will help make your home a better investment for your family.

You will be better off if you buy the right house, the home that will be best for you now, at this stage of your life and into the immediate years that follow. Your housing budget will be your starting point. You won't know what you should buy until you know how much you can spend on your home.

As you consider your options be open-minded. Start with a wide-open search of all possible homes. This will show you different property types that are available to you. Think of it as window-shopping, research and planning for your big investment. Look at the pros and cons of the different property types. After you know what options are available, you will narrow your search down to the property types you like and will consider buying.

Make a list of the needs and wants you have for your housing. List everything. Think about your lifestyle and your daily activities. Think about how you spend your time and in which rooms you spend most of your time. Do you spend a lot of time at home or are you out a lot? What are the things you like and dislike about the housing you have had so far in your life?

Your first home will not be your dream home. It is not meant to be. When custom homes are built the owners design them specifically for their lifestyle and needs. Yet even so,

> **FOOD FOR THOUGHT**
>
> **You should spend as much time evaluating the location as you do in evaluating which house you want.**

after they move in they likely will tell you there is something they would do differently. There is no such thing as a perfect house, but your goal should be to get as close as you can to a home that is perfect for you.

Remember to be realistic; do not expect your home to have every single thing you want. Use your list of needs and wants to narrow down your home choices. Get rid of the homes that don't meet your needs. Compare the homes left on your list with your wants and needs to determine your best options. There is more than one house that will be a good choice, but you will likely have a favorite that you will make an offer on first.

Real Estate Street Smarts

One of your wants or needs is not to pay too much for the home. Use the information on determining market value in chapter four to evaluate what price is a fair market price for the home. If the seller will not be reasonable you will have to decide if the value is a want or a need. In chapter ten you will learn all about negotiating contracts, the process and options available to you.

Your list of needs should be very basic items such as location, minimum size of living space, bedrooms, bathrooms, lot size, family room space or garage space as examples. Anything can be a need. For a person that cannot do stairs a main floor laundry, bathroom, bedroom, and kitchen are a must. With both the needs and wants lists you can rate each item from important, not important, just dreaming and everything in between. You can use a number or star system if you wish.

It is important to review your list as you look at homes and consider your options. It will keep you on track and help you avoid an emotional or pressured decision to buy something that does not meet your needs and lifestyle. Let me explain with this example. As a buyer you walk through a home that catches your eye. It is beautiful! Granite countertops, crown moldings, fancy cabinets, fixtures and appliances. The condition is just out of sight. The finish materials are much more expensive than the other homes you have seen and the layout of the home is great. But the home doesn't meet all your needs.

Don't let a few items from your wants and dream list push out your need list items. Keep in mind the whole picture. You can add upgrades later to a home in the right location with the right yard and layout for your lifestyle, but you can't change how far away your remodeled home is from where you work. As you can see you would enjoy the home more and be willing to stay longer if it meets your basic requirements first. Later on, when you have the money, you can improve your property to include more of the items from your list. If your home does not meet your basic needs you will not be happy or content and you will want to move.

Your list should identify which items can be changed and which items are not cost effective to change. You can actually move a home from one lot to another, but

---

FOOD FOR THOUGHT

At the very least you should look at 10 homes before you buy one. If you like the first home you see and want to make an offer before someone else does, make the offer. While you wait for an answer and in the days that follow during your inspection period go see more homes to make sure you picked the right one.

it is expensive. You can take down walls and change the layout of the home but it is also expensive. Items like moldings, flooring, cabinets, and painting are items that are easily done with costs that make sense (in many situations but not all). Painting is the most affordable change. Moldings and flooring cost more but are usually affordable. Cabinets can be expensive but do not require structural changes with additional cost.

You don't make money on the changes made to your home or on the maintenance of the home. You do not get an increase in sales price to match the amount you spend when you sell. Buyers expect a roof that works and flooring that is not worn out. If you put in new items it helps you sell your home and will increase your value from what it was, but does so based on the value it brings to a buyer and not on the cost of the improvement.

Kitchens, bathrooms, and decks recover the cost best and can increase the value beyond the cost in some cases. Pools in many parts of the country are on the other end of the spectrum for cost and value. If you want a pool you are better off buying a home that has a nice pool already. Putting in a pool may cost you $30,000 or more, but you may be able to find a home with an existing pool for minimal to no additional cost. Because of the cost and liability, a pool has no value to some buyers and even a negative value for others.

> ### FOOD FOR THOUGHT
>
> **Financially you are better off when you find a home that already has what you want. Many home improvements do not add 100% of their cost to the dollar value of your home.**

It is advantageous to buy a home that has what you want. Consider the time it takes and the inconvenience involved in home improvements. Time is money. Time is opportunity. It better be worth your time if you take on a project.

Your wants and needs list should factor in basic day to day convenience and quality of life components. Simple things are important, like the distance from where you park your car to your kitchen. You will be carrying grocery bags from your car to the kitchen after shopping on a regular basis. How many stairs do you have to go up or down to get there? Are you protected from the weather in a carport or a garage, or are you in the rain and snow?

Maybe having windows in your kitchen and family room that view your fenced back yard, so you can keep an eye on your kids while you are doing daily tasks, will be a big deal for you. Or it could be having a laundry room by the kitchen or by the bedrooms.

Real Estate Street Smarts

Let's brainstorm about things that you might care about.

Location: Where do you spend most of your time, or where do you want to spend most of your time? Think about work, play, and everything in between. There are many factors that you will consider: Location to church, schools, shopping, entertainment, and other services, the overall feel of the community, crime levels, airports, libraries, transportation systems, air quality, and geological risks of the area.

Within the same neighborhood there are significant differences in location. A cul-de-sac or dead-end street is more private than a regular residential street. A busy street that feeds traffic to the neighborhood or other neighborhoods nearby is also very different.

On the same street locations are different. Proximity to ditches, train tracks, commercial space, parks, bus stop, or other roads change the feel and use of the location. Homes on the same street also face different directions and are affected by the sunlight and the shade differently. West facing homes provide shade in the back of the home in the evening when most people spend time in their yard. In climates with snow, west facing front walks and driveways melt faster than north or east-facing areas that are shaded much of the day. South facing walkways and driveways also melt faster. You can test this yourself by paying attention to the homes on any street during winter. North and east facing homes require more work to remove snow and ice.

Pay attention to the surroundings of the neighborhood for anything that would affect the enjoyment of the home. Proximity to landfills, sewer treatment plants, animal farms, power sub stations, and other commercial property uses, to name a few. You will want to canvas the area in person and search on the web to check the surrounding area. The County Recorders Office and City Offices are also great resources. Smells, noise and traffic will affect your enjoyment of the neighborhood.

Consider the cost of commuting as you plan which locations are best for you. You will have daily time costs, car fuel costs, and added car repair costs from the additional use. These costs can vary, they could go up, but a fixed rate mortgage will not go up. It may be more affordable monthly to pay more for your home and less on your fuel and other travel related expenses.

FOOD FOR THOUGHT

Check online for information on the neighborhood such as crime, sex offenders on the registry and other statistics for the area.

Links are available at www.RESmartMoves.com

Real Estate Street Smarts

   Development type: What type of neighborhood is best for you? Developers have different ideas for communities they build. Some have no rules and some have many. Some have large lots with homes more spread out and secluded. Some developments have very small lots with homes close together. Some include community parks and other open space for the use of the residents.

   Some developments have amenities for the community to use including pools, playgrounds, tennis courts, golf coarse, clubhouses, horse stables, boat and RV parking, and pretty much anything else a developer can dream of that they think buyers will value. There are properties of all types where the HOA takes care of all the landscaping.

   These parks, pools, clubhouses, landscaping etc., even private roads in some cases are maintained and paid for by the HOA. The homeowners pay for everything the HOA has to do. If the HOA does not have enough money saved from the monthly HOA payments for a repair or improvement they charge each homeowner an assessment for their portion of the bill.

It is important to know what you are getting yourself into. **Check out the HOA!**

   Developments with HOA's come in all types. Everything from high rise apartments to Planned Unit Developments with single family homes on large lots. Many new neighborhoods have an HOA to help keep the consistency of the neighborhood and help keep it looking good in the future.

   A concern in developments with no HOA can be that the owners can do what they want and you may not like it. When you sell potential buyers may or may not like it either. The same is true for the HOA, with some buyers liking and not liking the rules and the costs.

   There are so many options and variations to consider. Farms, ranches, estates, suburban homes, twin-homes, townhouses, and condo's. Gated communities, mountain homes, mixed-use walkable communities, lake front property, and one type you may not know about, a co-op. A stock cooperative is real estate owned by a company for the purpose of controlling who lives in the development. The owners have stock in the company and as a part of their ownership they are granted a proprietary lease to live in their condo or house.

   The big difference on a cooperative is that a potential buyer would have to be approved by the co-op before they can buy into the company and be granted the lease. The buyer is required to provide financial and other information as part of the process. The buyer could be turned down by the co-op and not be able to move forward. With a normal real estate purchase only the homeowner has the right to say no to a buyer. Usually the seller is motivated by the ability of the buyer to purchase and is not interested in the details a co-op would be considering.

   As you can imagine for some people a co-op would be very desirable because of their desire to be around other people like them. It is a way for them to have more control and in some cases more privacy.

Property type: Single-family homes come in many styles, sizes and shapes.

Ramblers are great for people who want and need to avoid stairs because everything you need is all on the main level. Ramblers usually have 2, 3, 4 or more bedrooms on the main level. Ramblers over 1500 square feet on the main level often offer formal living room and family room space. Smaller ramblers likely have a living room or a family room and not both. Larger ramblers are more likely to have laundry rooms and half baths on the main level. In some areas these homes are allowed to have a lower basement level. On a rambler most of the basement is in the ground. In basements you likely will find game rooms, bedrooms, bathrooms, family rooms, storage rooms, utility rooms, cold storage rooms, and laundry rooms.

Ramblers come in many different layout options. They are popular because of their open floor plans, vaulted ceilings, and convenient garage space and access to the kitchen.

Two-Story homes have two levels above ground. They may have a basement level similar to the rambler. Two-story homes can also be similar to a rambler layout on the main level. Some have a bedroom and a full bath on the main level, and in some cases a master suite with a master bath, walk in closet, and master bedroom. The kitchen, dining, living room, family room, laundry, entry, and other specialty rooms depending on the size of the home are all on the main level. Some two-story homes do not have a bedroom or full bath on the main level, but may have a half bath.

Up a full flight of stairs, usually three to five bedrooms with two to three bathrooms and in some cases a laundry room, loft, or play room are all on the upper level. There can be variations that are only limited to the builders and owners imagination and wallet.

Two-story homes separate the

FOOD FOR THOUGHT

A half bath, a sink and a toilet, on the main level is great when you have company over because you don't have to send them to your kids or your own bathroom. Half baths are common for many house styles.

---

bedrooms from the entertaining and family space in the home. This comes with a flight of stairs, going up and down to get to bedrooms, but provides privacy and separation if it is wanted. Because the total size of the home is in two or three (if there is a basement) separate areas these plans improve in open feel and comfort as the size of the home increases. You would likely start looking seriously at them when you have homes with about 1,800 or more square feet on the two levels above ground.

The entry and other parts of the main level can be very grand with two story tall ceilings. Because there is another level the footprint of the home takes less yard space. They can fit on smaller lots and would provide more yard space on any lot.

Multi-level homes have four or more levels, and if the home has three levels it is called a **Tri-level**. Multi-level homes have many different designs and types. Generally they include an entry, formal living room, kitchen, and dining room on the main level. Some have a laundry room or a half bath also on the main level. Vaulted ceilings are very common for the main level giving an open feel to the home.

From the main level you have stairs going to the upper level where two to three bedrooms including a master suite on some homes, and one to two bathrooms. From the main level you usually have half a flight of stairs (7 stairs or so) to a family room. These family rooms are usually large with an open and connected feel to the main level with only a railing between the dining room and kitchen area to the family room. Off of the family room some homes have utility rooms, bedrooms, bathrooms, and laundry rooms. The family room level is directly under the bedroom level. If the home has 4 levels you go from the family room down half a flight of stairs to a basement that is under the main level of the home. On this level you will find a bedroom or two and a bathroom. Some layouts have utility rooms, storage rooms, game rooms, media rooms or other specialty rooms.

These homes are most appealing for buyers looking for homes that are 1500 to 2800 square feet. With 500 to 700 square feet on each level the room sizes are very good and the open and connected feel are very good compared to other homes of the same size. Along with other styles, having 3 bedrooms together is a plus for families with young kids. Many children don't feel comfortable far away from their parents until they get a little older. These plans provide separation from bedrooms and main level space. There is not a bedroom on the main level making this type unappealing for those buyers who can't or do not want to do stairs often.

Split Entry homes are similar to ramblers with important differences. On a split entry your front door is in your stairway. From your, usually small, entry you must go up or down a half a flight of stairs. The rooms and layout are very similar to a rambler. These plans are popular in areas that require the home to be further out of the ground than a rambler would be. On these plans the basement level is half in the ground and half out of the ground. The advantage is more daylight and better basement feel.

Attached garages on these homes do not have convenient access to the kitchen area of the home. Some enter the basement level and some are not accessible to the inside of the home.

These plans are most common with homes that are smaller than 2800 square feet. With the trends changing to large basement windows with large window wells this style has become less popular for buyers and builders.

 Variations of these types include what I call a **one and a half story** home which is basically a rambler with all the rambler rooms on the main level and the look from the curb of a rambler but it has an upstairs in the roof system using attic space. The upper level is usually half the size or less of the main floor and can include family rooms, bedrooms, and bathrooms. With these plans the top portion of the walls take an angle to the ceiling to give space for the roofline. The upper level space is usually full of character and could be described as a good use of the space. The down side is that some closets and other parts of the room are limited because of the angle of the roof and the low head clearance.

Building codes dictate how high the wall must be before it takes an angel to the ceiling. This is illustrated with a picture of an attic room before sheetrock.

Other homes like **A-frame** homes are similar to these other styles with the main difference of having the roof start very low to the ground level and extend steeply to the peak of the roof one to two stories higher.

Cabins can be of any style but are separated because of the rustic and natural materials used to build the structure and finish the home. A real log cabin is literally solid logs that are fitted and fastened together to support the structure and to provide the look desired on the inside and outside of the home. These logs settle in on themselves over time. A good design will allow for this to happen around windows without damage to the window and will provide large bolts that are used to adjust the home as needed.

There are also log veneer products that look like log but are for decoration on the outside of a stick frame structure much like many brick, rock, stucco, or siding would be applied to the outside of a home.

Twin-homes are homes sold separately but are connected to another home by one common wall. These can be any style and usually have their own yard. They are the step between a single-family home by itself and a townhouse that is connected to other units on each side with smaller yard space. It is not a duplex that must be sold together. A duplex is two units connected to each other and owned as one property by a landlord for rental income.

There are many different architectural styles including Modern, Victorian, Spanish, Colonial, Tudor, Conventional, Split, Bungalo, Basement, Cape Cod, Contemporary, and Ranch styles. Architectural differences affect the look, layout and use of a home.

Condo's, another major category to think about. Condo's all have an HOA and thus an HOA fee that is usually, but not always, due monthly. Condo's are different, some are PUD, Planned Unit Developments, and some are not. With a condo you need to know if the owner of the condo owns the outside of the building and is responsible for the maintenance of the exterior or if the HOA owns, maintains, insures and controls the exterior. There are variations of this. You will want to ask how the condo is set up and get a copy of the rules and bylaws to review during your inspection period.

A **Townhouse** is a condo that could be of any style but is joined with multiple other town homes on one or both sides. They do not have neighbors above or below them like a traditional condo or a high-rise condo. Of all condos this style is the closest you can get to a single-family home sitting on its own lot. These units may even have garages attached to them and often have a little private yard for their own personal use. An end unit only has one common wall. This shared wall is often actually two walls on newer units to provide noise reduction and further separation of the units. A middle unit has neighbors on both sides. End units give the opportunity for more windows and daylight in the home.

HOA costs and amenities vary widely to meet many different homeowner needs. A popular trend in condo developments are to include pools, basketball courts, tennis courts, work-out rooms, large gathering rooms, grass areas, and playground equipment as part of the HOA.

People who do not want to take care of a yard find the hassle free lifestyle appealing. The HOA for the development likely takes care of all exterior maintenance including cutting the grass. In the small private yards that are fenced the homeowner is required to care for that area.

Townhouses are usually 1400 to 2400 square feet and provide the space with lower land cost which allow a lower total cost for the living space.

Condo's have the feel of an apartment with the difference of home ownership. For some, condos are a starting point to get into the market because it is the most affordable land option available. The land price is low because of how many units sit on the same piece of land. These vary widely from three-story buildings to incredibly tall high-rise buildings. In areas with lower land costs, traditional condos tend to have more personal space with exterior access to your unit and are likely three stories tall (that is a lot of stairs to climb carrying groceries). Some condos emphasize affordability, some are luxury penthouse suites with lavish finish and amazing views. Like other home types you will find everything from small and basic to large and extravagant.

High-rise condos are convenient with elevators, interior hallways,

and in some cases security staff and systems. All residents come in on the main level to access their condo. Some condos have a balcony or two that offer fresh air and a little personal space outside.

With a condo you have neighbors below you and or above you. On the top level you have neighbors below and to each side. The views are

better from the top floor and you likely have vaulted ceilings that are not available on the lower levels. In middle units you have neighbors on all sides. The up side for this level is fewer stairs to climb and lower utility costs. Ground floor units do not have anyone below them. This is ideal for families with small children because of noise concerns for anyone below you. Bottom floor units are also best for those who have a hard time with stairs if the development does not have an elevator. In any case you must be okay with more walking to get to your unit from outside.

Parking comes in all types with covered and uncovered parking. Some even have garage space for the owners. More common parking is covered parking in the basement level or a carport outside. Condo's are a great way to improve neighborhood feel and amenities at a lower cost.

Year built: How old the home is could be an issue for you. When homes are built they are built to the current building codes. City or County inspectors check the progress during construction at key times to check for structural, system, safety, and finish requirements before they will give an occupancy permit to the owner or builder. These building codes are modified to make homes safer and better.

FOOD FOR THOUGHT

City zoning dictates how many units can be built on any piece of land. The more dense the zoning is, the more the land is worth. If you buy property before the zoning is changed by anticipating the necessary growth of a city or town, the value of your land will increase.

Have you ever been in a new house that had stairs that were very narrow and steep like you find in some homes that are one hundred years old? The building codes dictate how many inches a riser and a stair tread must be and have minimum requirements for staircase width.

Electrical systems have changed over the years and the code has changed with it. The current system is a grounded system with GFCI, Ground Fault Circuit Interrupters, required in areas using water and in other locations in the home. These are designed to protect people and the system from electrical shock.

The materials used and the methods of framing have changed over the years. Wood blocking is nailed to the roof framing and to the outside wall to tie the two together. Metal hurricane straps connect the cement foundation walls to the wood framing on top of it securing the two together. Proper ventilation for exhaust gas from, and fresh air to, the heating equipment keep the air inside the home safe.

Smoke and carbon monoxide detectors are wired together throughout the home to sound an alarm when unsafe conditions arise inside the home. When they are wired together they will all go off when one detects a problem, so if you have a fire on the upper floor you will hear about it in the basement.

Real Estate Street Smarts

A great example of changes made to the building codes that has made homes more safe and has improved the use and enjoyment of the living space is the change from the 1960's basement window size requirements to the current window size minimums. New homes and homes built in the 1980's have much larger basement windows. More daylight makes the space brighter and less like a dungeon. The larger windows also allow better access outside in the event of a fire or other emergency. The code also requires basement window wells to have ladders to climb out of the well. Don't panic if you fall in love with an older home, you can cut the concrete and install larger windows, problem solved.

I have noticed that significant changes come about every ten years or so as new products become available and as we learn from the experiences Mother Nature gives us.

I feel that building codes are your friend and we should be happy to comply with them. I will admit there are a few that seem very silly, like the requirement to have a railing if the top stair is an inch or two into a hallway or room. As if we would fall not expecting the stairs to start two inches before the wall.

An older home may have been updated to new codes if work has been done on a remodel, addition, an update or otherwise. You would need to check with the homeowner or the city to know. Many old homes have new plumbing, electrical, and heating systems. The County Records should show if changes have been made with a permit.

Convenience and style come with age. Builders build what current buyers are liking, asking for, and buying. These trends change as we change how we use our homes. New homes offer the most current lifestyle and in some cases allow the owner to shape the design to their own personal lifestyle. This comes at a price. In most cases new construction is more expensive than existing homes for sale.

I would like to point out some local trends that demonstrate this point. In the years prior to the depression, late 1880's to early 1900's, more homes had ten foot ceilings with more elaborate finish work, but during the depression many people did not have the money for non essential items so you end up with shorter ceilings, smaller and fewer moldings in the home. Extra features are just not necessary, these homes are much more basic in comparison. The early to mid 1900's cellars or crawl spaces and wannabe basements with short ceilings and unplanned layouts gave way in the 1970's to much more appealing basements with well planned rooms, better ceiling height, and a finish similar to the main level of the home--not as an after thought, but planned living space for the home.

In the 1980's master suites with master bedroom, master bathroom, and walk in closets became popular. Single-pane windows gave way to double-pane windows.

Real Estate Street Smarts

Carports of the 70's became garages in the 80's. By the 1990's two-car garages became standard on even the smallest of homes. Built in entertainment centers and media rooms were popular with a two-foot recess for your big screen TV. Starting in the 80's but really making ground in the 90's came the return to open vaulted ceilings and higher ceilings as our nation prospered. In the 1990's three or more garages were likely to be found in homes in the five thousand square foot range or larger. Aluminum windows were replaced by vinyl windows for the bulk of housing. (Homeowners liked the aluminum windows when they changed from the wood windows of the early and mid 1900's.)

From 2000 until 2007 we had incredible prosperity and it shows in the housing trends. Three thousand square-foot homes and larger, likely

FOOD FOR THOUGHT

Demand drives trends. If no one buys, Builders and Owners will change until people do.

have three-car garages attached to them. Many townhouses have one and two-car garages attached. We must all have a ton of stuff we want to keep out of the weather. Or maybe we want it out of sight and secured, to keep it from being stolen.

Most homes have nine-foot, ten-foot tall or vaulted ceilings. Nine-foot ceilings are now popular in basements. The finish work is more elaborate once again. Hand textured walls similar to the look many decades ago, replaced the orange peel spray on texture that was so popular in the 70's, 80's, and 90's. With the invention of the flat screen TV hanging on walls all over America the two-foot recess built ins for entertainment centers are long gone.

Basic housing offered with high-end finish work, such as granite or solid surface countertops, tile and wood floors are commonplace.

2008 and 2009 show similar trends with one noticeable difference. Our Nation's economy and housing market are in recession and the building industry has been hit hard. Builders are filling the need for affordable and attractive pricing to motivate buyers into new homes. Builders are now emphasizing smaller, more affordable home plans and a more basic level of finish to start with at their base price. Buyers may upgrade the home at their expense.

National trends show that peo-

FOOD FOR THOUGHT

Homes built during the boom years reflect the attitudes of the day. Bigger and better is best and money seemed to grow on trees. Builders now are spending less because buyers are spending less.

ple are starting to buy smaller homes now. The size of homes had been increasing for years.

The size of homes will likely continue to get a little smaller as we all have a reality check after the booming years of prosperity and building more space than we need. Floor plans of tomorrow will adapt to the new lifestyle of the next generation integrating convenience and technology with rooms designed for multiple functions. We have gone wireless. The days of running networking wires are all but over.

Looking into the future I expect high energy costs to drive demand for more expensive, more efficient, heating and air conditioning systems instead of the least expensive systems available. The least expensive systems available are regulated to meet a minimum requirement but there are many options to upgrade your equipment to make it more efficient and save money on your utility bills.

When the energy costs are high enough, buyers will demand better systems and builders will start giving consumers what they want. Right now the extra cost is not justified for the builder.

With brand new homes the owner often will also have the cost and time needed to complete landscaping. It is common for builders to only put in the landscaping that the development requires upon completion of the home and in some cases they even have the buyer complete the landscaping requirement by doing it themselves or paying an upgrade cost to have it done for them.

With land costs high in some areas, lot sizes have been trending to smaller lots even for large homes. An advantage of an older home is not only location but also the chance of a larger lot at an affordable price.

With an older home you get the advantage of mature trees and landscaping. When you buy an older home you have a history of how well or bad the soil conditions have been for the home. Problems such as settling, flooding, wind damage and home system problems can be inspected and evaluated. On a new home you don't know for sure. You need to evaluate the builder, sub contractors, and the soil to even have a clue what you are getting.

With older homes the neighborhood is what it is, what you see is what you get and it will not likely be changing any time soon.

In a new neighborhood a dead end street can become a through street later. A beautiful view can get blocked. A wonderful future park or promised amenity may not happen.

Personality and history are huge reasons to buy an older home. The character and the attention to detail drive

> **FOOD FOR THOUGHT**
> The age of a home does not make it good or bad, it is the care and the quality when it was built and how it was maintained that make the difference.

some buyers to older homes. Prices can also drive demand of older homes but old homes with character that were built and maintained with care provide the owner with a great lifestyle and sense of pride much like the owner of a newly built custom home.

Layout of the home: What rooms do you need? Where do you need them to be and how big do they need to be? What is important to you, function, uniqueness, separation, open feel, or flow? There are so many floor plans out there that you will just have to feel out what you like and don't like by looking at different floor plans in your price range until you know what works best for you. Viewing one of each style before you cross it off your list is not hard to do. You may have been inside many different styles already.

Different layouts are better at different stages of life. If you plan on keeping the home for a very long time you will need to think ahead of the current stage of life you are in.

Young people with small children likely want 3 bedrooms close together, usually on the same level of the home and a place for toys close by the main living rooms of the home.

When you have teenagers you will likely want some bedrooms separate from the master suite. Little children under 12 usually don't like these rooms on other levels of the home because of the perceived great distance away from mom and dad, but teenagers love it. I am told bedrooms and family room space away from mom and dad's room is because of the noisy teenagers, but I will let you decide on that.

Later on in life when your children are all gone the bedrooms on the same level as the master are changed to an office/library and a craft room. Convenient for daily access, both of you get your own hobby room. The teenager bedroom(s) usually end up as guest bedrooms for the occasional visit from your children and grandchildren. Grandparents love to have floor plans that have large open rooms, arranged together to accommodate large gatherings.

This description is not going to fit everyone of course but you would be surprised how many people have the same basic needs during their lives.

When you buy you are wise to think into the future and select a home that best meets your current and future needs. You have options as you get older. If you can't do stairs well you can install a motorized chair lift that folds up to the wall when you are not using it but will take you up the stairs when you do need it. It is a lot cheaper to add then the cost of selling and buying a home. It is not ideal compared to one level living though because of the potential to fall and get hurt.

Most people don't stay in the first home they buy, but many do stay in their second or third home.

Real Estate Street Smarts

After you choose your home think of ways you can improve the use of the space you have. How can you arrange furniture to maximize the space and increase the appeal and comfort of the room? Consider built in shelves and storage to increase your space. On inside walls this can even be done without changing wall studs. Be creative to find solutions to problems the layout creates for your family. Customize your home to fit your lifestyle and express yourself.

I can promise you when you look at homes you will see layouts that make you think to yourself "who, in their right mind would want the layout this way?" The answer to that question is at least one. All it takes is one builder, or one homeowner and there you go.

Do you need to think about what will be appealing for resale? Yes or no depending on your situation. If you want to limit your investment risk or possibly increase the return on your investment you should factor that in. If you are thinking purely about a great place to live and that you are not likely to ever sell you would not worry about what other people want. If it is a factor for you don't guess, look it up! You can have your realtor pull sold statistics for layout and property types in your price range and area to show you what most people are buying.

You may find that you also like the same things many other people find valuable and when you go to sell your home, it will appeal to more people. If your home is so unique to your taste that it is not appealing to other buyers you will end up dropping your price to entice a buyer. The buyer will buy because of the good price. A "unique" home will often sell for the price of a home that is significantly smaller.

Land or lot size: How much time do you spend outside? How important is privacy to you? How much money do you have? The third question along with what location you want to live in may answer the first two questions for you. If price is not a problem you will need to consider a few things about yard size.

Landscaping does not take care of itself. It will cost you either time, money or both. It also provides great benefit and may be worth much of both.

There are so many things you can do with land. Room to have outbuildings such as a shop, extra garage space or basketball pad, tennis court, grass, gardens, gazebo, swing sets, playgrounds, tree houses, ponds, sand boxes, pathways, fire pits, water features, hot tubs, pools, greenhouse and pretty much anything you can dream of that the city, county, and HOA will allow.

The bigger your yard the more it will cost you and the more it will provide for you. If you do not want much to take care of or if you are not the type to go outside much you can get the privacy you want with the purchase of a good set of blinds for your home.

Real Estate Street Smarts

In populated areas land is expensive and small lots are commonplace. Builders and developers split raw land into the smallest possible sizes to fit the required set backs for the homes to be built and the total lot size requirements for the city they are in.

Most subdivisions will have a general range of lot sizes. For example a subdivision may have lots from a third of a acre (.3) to a half of an acre (.5), from .2 to .4, or .1 to .25 in many new developments. Because they have to put roads through this raw land they end up with a variation of sizes in the neighborhood.

When builders and developers sell these lots or new homes on these lots they usually charge more, called a lot premium, for the better lots. Shape, size, and placement in the development go into this calculation. Buying the best lot you can afford is a great investment for your home. You cannot change this later so do the best you can. Whether you pay two thousand extra or if you pay 10% more on your land cost you have increased the value and enjoyment of your home much more than the dollar amount spent.

When you sell, a great lot will increase the value of your home based on the total price and you likely only paid a premium on the land value of the property. Land costs are usually 1/4 to 1/3 of the total cost of the home. If base price lots are going for ninety thousand and you paid nine thousand more for your lot to get the larger lot south or west facing on a non-through street away from the train tracks or highway you would have paid 10% more for the better location.

Buyers when they compare your great lot to a less appealing lot they will expect the less appealing property to sell for 10% less. The 10% difference is on total price, likely to be $300,000 or more for a home on a lot in that price range. So the $9,000 additional costs will increase your value approximately $30,000.

The logic is simple, a buyer spending approximately $300,000 for their home is willing to pay much more than $9,000 dollars to enjoy the better location. If the buyer wants to save money by buying the home with the less appealing location they want to save more than $9,000. No one will pick the less appealing location for a reduction of 3%, it is not worth it. Have you ever purchased anything that wasn't exactly what you wanted because it was 3% off? On a home if it is 10% less expensive buyers notice. It may take more. So it is safe to say the net gain for spending $9,000 upfront is $21,000 and the enjoyment while living there is a bonus.

You can check this fact by looking at sold information comparing great location, large lots, to lots on busy streets, next to train tracks, and small yards that limit use of back yard space. It should not be a surprise that buyers are willing to pay more for what they want on items that cannot be changed.

The key is to pick a well-priced development in a good location and pick the best possible lot in the development within your budget.

Many people are okay with yards that are not huge. Having a .2 acre lot with 40 feet off the back of the house works for many people. When you have 20 to 25 feet off the back of the home and in some cases even less, it limits the use of the space.

Lot sizes from .20 to .33 have great appeal for subdivision dwellers. More back yard space compared to front yard space is good. Adequate parking space and room on the side of the home to access the back yard are all important factors to consider.

Small yards are still yards. Even the small lots with .1, one tenth of an acre, do offer a private space for your enjoyment and are the right fit for some home buyers who do not want to pay more for additional yard space.

Utilities: You may not have a lot of choice with this one but you will likely run into a few homes that are built with different systems and types of fuel. In more remote locations that do not have the public sewer, gas, and possibly electricity, the systems will be different. Whether you care about the differences or not it is good to know a little about how they are different. The cost of running and maintenance can be very different.

Heating systems for the home are generally run on natural gas. Forced air units that have ductwork running from a furnace to all the rooms of the home are the most common. With these units central air conditioning connects into the furnace to take advantage of the vents, ductwork, and blower motor. The air conditioning unit sits outside and is usually an electric unit.

These systems are popular because of their cost and their ability to regulate comfortable temperatures throughout the home.

In some areas similar systems run off electricity or propane. Propane systems have a tank on site to supply the home. Trucks come and fill the tank. It is a good option when natural gas is not available.

Other heat systems include radiant heat that can be hot water heated and circulated though pipes in the floor or units attached to the wall. Floor systems provide a warm, comfortable floor even in the basement. Electric radiant systems are usually

---

FOOD FOR THOUGHT

If you don't like shoveling snow install a heated driveway and walkways then watch the snow melt away.

---

attached to the walls of the home. With radiant systems you can have different temperatures in each part of the home. All the radiant systems are appealing to people with allergies because they do not blow dust around the home.

There are homes that have been designed to take advantage of the natural heat of the sun, and the heating and cooling affect of the ground. These homes cost more to build and are not common. You can expect to pay more for the home but save on monthly utility costs.

Air conditioning in hot areas will be important. Swamp coolers, window units and roof-mounted systems are less expensive to run and to purchase. The down side is they do not flow evenly in the home so you will have cold and warm areas in the home and on humid days they do not work as well. Cool air comes from air blown through water soaked pads into the home. These units must be started up in spring and winterized during fall. They have a tendency to create water related damage and maintenance. Hardwood and carpet in the home don't appreciate the change in humidity. They also require cleaning where the air enters the home.

Electric central air is most common and most appealing generally for its ease and comfort throughout the home. Electric units can also be window or wall units that are designed for one room only. With these units you also have the hot or cold spots like other similar units.

Ceiling fans and whole house fans installed in the ceiling force air out of the attic space to keep the home cooler with airflow. They may be used on their own or with other cooling systems to reduce cost. It does not cool the air but moves the hot air out to replace it with new air. In the heat of the summer this will not work well on its own like a system that cools the air it is moving.

Waste management will vary based on the area. You will either have a septic tank and leach field on your property to break down waste or you will be on the public sewer system.   You own the plumbing from the street to and through the house, and the city owns the plumbing from the street to the sewer treatment plant. You pay monthly for public sewer use.

With a private septic system you own and maintain the system entirely. It requires maintenance that can include additives to help break down the waste or, when necessary, removing the waste from the access point at the top of the tank by a company with the right equipment.

Wind and solar power are not common because of their cost, but will become more popular as they become more affordable. If you want to "live off the grid" you can find property with a septic tank, well for water, and you can use solar or other sources of electricity. The up side with these properties is that you are not on the grid if the grid has problems . This is appealing for people who want to be more self-sufficient. Most people are on the power grid with a local power provider.

The down side is it is more expensive to start off and if there is a problem with any portion of the process it is yours alone to fix. Solar and alternative power could change how developments are designed and where they are located in the future.

That should get you started thinking about what is important to you regarding your housing. Your wants and needs lists should be growing. You will not get everything you want but you will get a lot more of what you want because you are thinking about it and searching for the best possible housing.

Real Estate Street Smarts

-Chapter 10-
Get The Right Price, Negotiate Your Contract, Evaluate & Inspect Your Home.

You will do well in real estate when you buy right. That means the right house at the right time for the right price. Don't rush, do it right! When you find the right house you want to move quickly, right? Yes you do, but not before you are prepared to make an offer.

Evaluate the situation. Do you know what the situation of the seller is? Before you make an offer you should find out why the seller is selling. What is important to them? Is price the most important thing to them? How motivated are they? How soon do they need to sell? How long have they been on the market? Do they already have another home? How much time do they need to move? How much time do they need to respond to an offer? How did they price their home, high, low, or just right? How much less than list price on average are homes selling for in the area on a home that is priced right? How much is the home worth to you? Is there anything the seller needs or wants that we can put in our offer to make it appealing to the seller other than the price?

You should already have a lender letter to send with your offer. All sellers want to have confidence that their deal will close, so they can move. Another need of many sellers is to have a few days after the transaction has been recorded and is final, to finish moving out. Remember sellers don't know for sure they are moving until your loan, other funds, and paperwork are all completed and recorded. Transactions fall apart even after buyers and sellers have signed.

If you know the seller has another house and has moving dates for the new house you can gain favor with them by conforming to their timing needs. You can look at items on the contract that don't cost you much that will make the seller happy and increase your ability to get a lower price. Timing that works well for the seller is only one thing, there are many items that don't cost a lot. Look for ways to help the seller feel comfortable, and do it with items that will not cause a problem for you.

Earnest money is part of your down payment. At closing it is credited to you as money already paid toward the price of the home. Earnest money for your offer should be .5 to 1% of the purchase price. This will help put the seller at ease because if you do not follow the contract terms they are entitled to the earnest money. This makes them feel more secure because they would receive money to cover a months mortgage payment and other costs, if you go to the end of the contract and cannot or will not close, leaving them with a house they thought they sold. At least they would have the money to pay the payment for the month and could get it back on the market. An offer with very little earnest money does not offer this security for them.

Real Estate Street Smarts

This is a great way to make the seller feel good about your offer at no increased cost to you for the home. As long as you follow the terms of the contract you do not lose any of this money. Read your contract carefully so you know what you can and cannot do. Look for an evaluation period with refundable earnest money to inspect the home. Some contracts, not to pick on builders, do not have evaluation periods with totally refundable earnest money. Most builders give you a week after reserving your lot to evaluate the purchase and sign a contract. They give you time to secure financing and then require a complete commitment that may include large deposits above earnest money.

The state approved contracts in Utah allow for a time period for the buyer to evaluate and back out for any reason and keep all their earnest money. You must notify the other party in writing within the deadline. There are also loan denial conditions and appraisal conditions on most offers.

If you are denied a loan you can cancel your contract with the seller. If the appraisal does not come in at purchase price or higher you may cancel the contract or you may ask the seller to reduce the price to the appraised amount. You cannot

---

FOOD FOR THOUGHT

When you make your offer compliment the sellers home and express your love for the home. Focus on positive things about the house in your communication. Remember if there is a problem it is the price not the house. Sellers have an emotional attachment to the home, but not the price. If you talk down their house they will take it personally and will feel less motivation to negotiate favorably with you.

Tell the seller at the time of the offer that you are prepared to secure financing for the home, as evident by the lender letter included with the offer, and that the home is a perfect fit for you.

Sellers want someone to live in their home that care for it as much as they did. This will go a long way. Don't lie, if you don't like the house why in the world would you buy it? So I think it is safe to pay the seller these compliments. Another advantage you can give yourself is by painting a picture of you or your family by telling them a little about you so when they review your offer they are thinking about a nice hard working family that loves their house. This is one reason why a seller's agent will keep distance between the buyer, and their client, the seller. If you do not have any direct contact with the seller write this information on a short note with the offer.

force the seller to reduce the price but you may negotiate a price change. The buyer or seller may pay the difference from the purchase price and the appraised value, but the lender will not loan more than their agreed percentage of the appraised value or purchase price whichever is lower.

Because the sellers biggest concern is having the buyer fall through and not close, the earnest money amount on the contract and the pre-qualification letter from a reputable lender is very important to help the seller feel comfortable.

For no extra cost, but high affect on the seller, use contract deadlines that make the seller feel comfortable. These deadline suggestions are examples of a simple purchase of a residential home on a developed residential lot. If you are buying a farm or commercial property, they are more complicated and you will need more time for all of these deadlines. Consult with a professional for your specific situation.

Give the seller 3-5 days to get disclosures to you about the home. This will include information from the seller about the property and it will include a title report from the title company concerning the condition of title, and the commitment for title insurance. It may also include covenants conditions and restrictions, HOA meeting minutes and other information applicable to the property.

Have your inspection deadline 7-10 days from offer acceptance. This way you have the time you need to evaluate the home including having an independent inspector come out and test and inspect the home. Keeping this deadline short is important to the seller because the buyer can back out for any reason and keep the earnest money.

FOOD FOR THOUGHT

With the new federal guidelines for appraisals that started to take affect May 1st 2009 there is a middleman that takes in appraisal orders and assigns an appraiser. This has increased the time needed for the appraisal, loan denial, and closing. Adding a week to these dates may be necessary. Talk with your lender to find out how long appraisals and loan approvals have been taking.

In the past your appraisal and loan approval deadline could be 14 days after offer acceptance. In most cases, more time is needed to finish the loan approval process and finalize the loan. Check with your lender prior to making the offer to make sure they are comfortable with this deadline. 21-28 days is common in today's lending world.

If your lender is not comfortable with these deadlines you have some work to do before you make an offer. You need to prepare yourself so you can meet these deadlines. If your situation requires more time to improve credit scores, pay off debt or save more money you will need to wait to make an offer. The timing problem may be with the lender, and if it is, find a new lender. Talk to three different lenders to find out if they all feel the same way. If your loan file is borderline, (right on the line of acceptable and not acceptable), find out how far you can go toward approval before you have a contract to buy a home. You will need to give all your documentation to the lender so they can submit the file for approval.

Determine the time they will need for buyer due diligence deadlines. These deadlines are the time the buyer has to secure financing and make sure they are okay with the condition of the home and property. Remember if deadlines are too long the seller will not be comfortable and may counter-offer to change deadlines. If the seller has to counter-offer anyway they may as well ask for more money at the same time. Appealing deadlines will help you get the best possible price on the home.

Close in 30-45 days from acceptance. Sellers usually don't want to wait a long time. This is plenty of time to complete the transaction. Ask the sellers what their plans are and what timing will work best for their situation.

Double check deadline and closing requirements with your lender before you make your offer. You are bound by your contract but your lender is not. It is up to you to feel comfortable that your lender will get your loan done by the closing/settlement deadline. The above dates can vary a little depending on the situation. The idea here is to have dates that work for you but are appealing to the seller.

Before you make an offer you should check to see how much they owe on their home. This will let you know if they have the option of going down on their

---

FOOD FOR THOUGHT

If you need to extend the closing date with the seller find out exactly what has happened, what needs to happen, and how long it will take. Explain the situation in detail to the seller. By doing this in detail the seller will be more likely to extend the contract for you.

Sellers feel comfortable with changes when they understand what is happening. If they don't know what is going on they will feel like they are wasting their time with you.

price and it will also tell you if money is tight for the sale of the home. It is possible that the seller could not close the transaction by owing more than they would receive from selling the home. They could end up in breach of the contract with you for not selling and you would be left without a house to move into after spending money evaluating the home, preparing your loan and making moving plans. Don't forget the costs the seller has as you estimate this. You will not know how much they are paying so I would just estimate 7% total cost above the recorded loan amounts for Realtor commission and title/closing fees.

This loan information is recorded on the county records. In some counties this is easy to get online. If not, you will need to talk to a title company or go to the recorders office. If you have an agent you can have them do this for you. If the seller will not make enough off of the sale to pay for everything you can require in your offer proof of funds for the amount they are lacking to finalize the sale. This will help limit your risk of a failed transaction.

FOOD FOR THOUGHT

When you have an accepted contract with the seller, you will review what is recorded on title from the title company. Check the owners of record on title to make sure you have all their signatures to make a valid contract. If you don't have them all, the contract is not valid. Also check to see if the seller has any judgments against them since judgments must be satisfied in order to buy or sell a home.
<u>Read your title commitment from the title company.</u>

It is possible to have a sale transfer fee recorded, by a developer or previous land owner, on the property you are going to buy. It can be on title or in the CC&R's (Covenants, Conditions & Restrictions). These transfer fees are not legal in some states. In my home state of Utah it is currently allowed. A development in Salt Lake County has a transfer fee of one percent of the sales price that is paid every time the home changes hands for 99 years. This is just one more reason you need to read your title commitment (PR, Preliminary Report of the Public Records) and the entire CC&R's. If you have a transfer fee you will have to deal with it when you sell. I would ask the seller to pay it for you when you buy, and I recommend paying it for the buyer when you sell. Raising the out of pocket cost of buying your home will not help the situation.

What percent of the list price are homes selling for in the current market? The reason you check to see what is normal in the market, for offer price compared to list price, is simple. You want to get the best price possible. The seller knows the market because they have been in the market working to sell their home, and they will know the market well if they have hired a good agent. Many sellers are dreamers and want to test the market at a high price that is appealing to them. It is crucial that you check market value for yourself so you know how they priced the home. If they priced the home at a great price, (to sell the home quickly), and you submit a low offer you may lose out on the house or may end up paying more for the home because you upset the seller.

If homes are selling for 3% under list price on average and you offer them 20% less they are not likely to go for it if they have priced their home at market value. But, if you offered the average 3% under list price on a home that is priced too high, you would be paying too much for the home.

If it is a buyers market they will expect a buyer not to offer full price. They would also know how much lower, on average, homes are selling for. A question you need to ask is if the seller has any offers on the home? Have they had any offers on the home before? If so what was the problem with the previous offer(s)?

If there is another offer on the home, find out when they need to respond to the other offer. If they have a really long time, like two weeks, or if they have a vague response time, the offer is not likely to be a good one. If it is an offer they need to respond to in a few days, you will need to offer with the expectation that you will only have one chance at it. So you would not give them a low-ball offer. You would likely offer them what you would have been happy to negotiate to, if you had started with a lower offer to see what they say. By asking the seller if they are offering any incentives you can find out if the seller is firm on their listed price or if they are flexible.

If you are the only offer, you would estimate what the home is worth to you, then calculate what you think the seller is expecting, based on the information you have gathered. If the value of the home, to you, is more than what the seller expects, negotiations are likely to be successful. Start with an amount that is less than what you think the seller is expecting. The closer you are to the amount the seller will accept, the more likely you are to get the best possible price. If you offer is close to the seller's bottom line they may just take it. If the home has been on the market for a long time, (months and months), with no price reductions you should be more aggressive. If they have not been on the market long, the seller will not feel desperate. You can either make a better offer, or likely, make a fair offer that they will only accept after a few months of first hand market education/experience.

Don't pay more than the home should be worth. Be honest in your evaluation so you can be successful. If in your negotiations with the seller they are above your estimated value, make a final offer, then when they don't want it, back off a little and give them space. You don't want to upset or make them angry you just want them to know the price is a problem for you.

Give them time. If you make an honest assessment of value, the market will teach the seller of the truth and they will call you a week or a month later to see if you are interested in the home.

For the seller, having an offer on the table and having it go away leaves them thinking about it. Who needs the other person more? Is there another house that the buyer likes as well? Is there another buyer that wants the sellers home? In a sellers market, the answer is that there are many buyers that want the home and that is why prices go up quickly.

In a buyers market, only the great properties that have been priced well will have more than one buyer at a time that wants them. All the overpriced homes get little to no attention.

If you are more motivated to buy a steal of a deal, than you are motivated to buy a certain house, you will need to make offers like an investor. To get the deal you want you will need to make many offers to find the one seller that is motivated to give you your price. You need to know what is more important to you. The deal or the details of the home, and there are situations where the deal is more important for the buyer. A word of caution in this situation, avoid a seller that is motivated because of issues with the home, and look for a motivated seller that is motivated because of their personal situation, like job change or job loss. A home that has problems will not sell well unless the problems are resolved. Some problems cannot be changed easily.

You, as a buyer, need to determine the value. Do not leave this to the seller and the seller's agent. Trust me, you don't want to leave it to an appraiser either. You will want their advice and perspective but <u>you should determine what the home is worth to you.</u>

Appraisers have the job of giving a professional opinion of value to help a lender or the person who hired the appraiser to justify a transaction amount. Is the value suggested confirmed by recent sold properties that are similar? Similar is a relative term isn't it? The opinions of appraisers vary just as the opinions of real estate professionals do. I have heard sellers agents tell me, when I told them their price was 15% too high, that they had an appraiser that could get this done for us. NO THANKS!

Recently changes have been made to the appraisal industry to try to help with this problem of agents or lenders working with appraisers who will appraise homes for the prices requested, even if it is not justified. Now the lender orders an appraisal from a third party. They no longer have direct contact with the appraiser. The third party selects which appraiser they will send out on the job. This will likely help reduce loan fraud problems, but does create some problems of its own. Appraisers and lenders have concerns about how it affects them in their day-to-day business. Time will tell if this helps as much as regulators are hoping, or if it will just create new problems.

If you buy a home that is priced 15% too high you will likely be in the home for at least five years before it is worth what you paid for it. If you need to sell too soon, you can see what a risk and liability this creates for you. You would be better off renting in this situation, or better yet, find a realistic seller to buy from.

Do yourself a favor and don't choke on two thousand dollars. If the home meets your needs, and it is your favorite house, you should not be troubled by a small amount if you are buying the home for five or more years. Also realize that really great houses sell for more than good houses. It is not like a car where you can look up the value in a book and plug in the condition, options, and mileage.

Two rounds in this sport! Did you know you have two opportunities to negotiate a contract? We just talked about the first one. Most of your negotiations should happen when you make your offer, but there is another opportunity to work out small but significant details. Your inspections provide you the opportunity to object to problems or concerns you find in your inspections. During the inspection period you can negotiate for the seller to lower the price to compensate for items, for the seller to take care of items, a mixture of the two, or you could get creative and ask for more included items. Anything you need modified could be negotiated at this point.

The big difference is that with the second negotiation opportunity, during inspections, the seller is not obligated to do anything for you. They do know that you can back out, so they may be willing to do more for you if they don't want to lose you. They also have the house sold in their mind so that works for you as well. It helps to have reasonable requests for reasonable inspection items. I have seen sellers that are very willing to be fair about repair issues but have also seen them react negatively (take a hike!) to unrealistic and unfair requests. Use common sense to evaluate the situation fairly.

In your first offer negotiations, if you know you are competing with another offer, or you want a low cost way to make the seller feel better about your offer price, you can offer to take the house how it is. Meaning that when you do your evaluations you will not ask for anything more from the seller. The risk you take, is that this puts you in a buy it or don't buy it situation if you find a faulty furnace or other expensive repair item.

Inspections.
After you have an accepted contract you will want to get right into your in-

spections to make sure this is the place for you. Take the time to go by the neighborhood at different times in the week, the day, and the night to see what people are up to and what the feel of the place will likely be when you move in.

After you buy, is not the time to find out that you can't stand the neighbors, or traffic, or noise, or smell.... you get the idea. Talk to the neighbors; ask them what they can tell you about the home and the property. Ask all adjoining neighbors if the property line is

FOOD FOR THOUGHT

Trust but verify your information. A trip to the city hall can answer your question on who owns the land next to yours, and it may even be available online. Check out our website at *www.RESmartMoves.com* for helpful links to the county recorder or your own cities web site.

correct as far as they understand it. Ask them what they like and don't like about the neighborhood. You will get all sorts of information. Remember to talk to multiple neighbors. Everyone needs one crazy person in the neighborhood to keep life interesting, but if there are too many... that would make you the crazy person, if you know what I mean.

If there is any undeveloped land, you can ask what they have been told about it's possible future use. You should get your information from the City and the County regarding vacant land located next to your potential home.

Don't get so attached to the house that you can't move on. Not until you have evaluated the home and closed on it. You will save yourself a lot of stress and money.

If you find a foundation problem or other defect that cannot be resolved with the seller, or if there is a sex offender living next door, and you don't want your kids that close, you need to be able to cancel and move on.

Have a home inspector, or at very least, a knowledgeable friend help you check the home. A home inspector is well worth the few hundred dollars you will spend to find out what you are getting. This can save you thousands later on, as I discovered first hand. As a young consumer (not an agent), with no knowledge of what I was doing, I purchased a home with a furnace that had to be replaced before the gas company would turn the gas back on to the home. It had a crack in the manifold and was dangerous. Carbon monoxide in a home can be deadly, so the gas company red tagged the furnace when they were out to check a gas leak outside on the gas meter. We did not live in the home yet but did spend time there remodeling the home in preparation to move in. This was a two thousand dollar surprise. A few hundred would have been a lot better for an inspector, he/she would have pointed out the crack in the manifold on the furnace and likely the cracked sewer line in the crawl space that was repaired later for a little over five hundred dollars. Both of these items are items a seller would be likely to fix or compensate a buyer for. Sellers are likely to repair legitimate problems.

If there is not a significant problem with the home you will be happy to know it and that alone is worth the inspection cost. Usually you start with a general home inspection unless you have a concern or know of something specific to check before spending money on the general inspection.

From the results of the general inspection you may decide to test for other things as well. There are many tests available to you. You can test for methamphetamines (meth), radon gas, lead paint for homes older than 1979, termites, asbestos, stucco exteriors, and mold. You can also note other items such as the amount of insulation in the home. You are likely to learn of many areas you can improve.

You will have items to evaluate that are outside of an inspector's inspection of the property, for instance is there any potentially hazardous waste on the property? Is the property located in a flood zone?

Are there any geological conditions that may threaten the home? A geologist can check soil make up for you and look at potential risks from spring run off water, creeks, rivers, lakes, mountains, ground water, soil composition and more.

Do you remember the high floodwaters in Washington County in southern Utah back in 2005? The river moved about 50 feet from where it was before. The local news showed horrifying video of homes falling into the river.

In 1983 a whole town was changed when a mudslide on the other side of the mountain dammed the Spanish Fork River and completely flooded and destroyed the town. It has never been the same.

The pictures that follow show you how the area is now.

Real Estate Street Smarts

Picture taken in 2009
Spanish Fork River

1983 mud slide
blocks river here

It was life altering for
the residents of Thistle.

Thistle

Real Estate Street Smarts

In 1976 in Idaho the Teton Dam broke, flooded seven towns, and damaged thousands of homes. Eleven deaths were attributed to the flood.

Failed Teton Dam, picture taken 2009

In 2005 a mudslide destroyed a four-unit townhouse building on the east bench of north Utah County. Southern Utah County also experienced a mudslide on its east bench in 2002. Mud stopped up a canal pushing water into homes nearby. These mud and floodwater damaged homes were not located by the lake or flood zones. A year before the mud slide their was a fire on the mountain above these homes. There were heavy rains the next year and without plants and trees to hold the dirt in place, there you go, you end up with a mudslide.

Look at the surrounding terrain to evaluate the geological impact and risk. Homes in many different locations have had spots of settlement and other soil and geological related risk. You will want to know about the surroundings and potential risks of the area. Every location will have some risk. Limiting your risk when you make investments is good financial planning.

Is the home located in an area with the possibility of falling rocks from the mountain above? Is the home in an area affected by earthquakes? Areas on or next to fault lines can have significant damage in an earthquake. Liquefaction of the soil is also a concern with an earthquake. These areas have soils that when they shake hard for a minute or more the soil condition allows buildings to settle and sink much like a marble on top of a jar of flower would sink into the flower when the jar is shaking. You can add earthquake coverage to your insurance policy.

Fire is a risk that can happen to anyone. You can look for safety problems with the electrical and others systems of the home. You can also follow safety guidelines to keep your risks down, like keeping paper and wood away from the furnace. You would be shocked how often people store flammable items next to their furnace. Candles, cooking oil, and cigarettes start their fair share of home fires. Fire should be covered by your insurance, check the terms to know how well you are covered. Don't forget about your belongings that will need to be replaced as well as replacing the home.

The location of the property can be a huge factor for fire risk. Each year in California fires threaten and destroy homes. History is a great indicator of the future. Taking the time to do a little research will go a long way.

Homes by busy streets may have car accident risks. You have seen those on the news, and I personally have been in two homes, that in their past, have had a car in their living space, by accident.

Insurance can help take some of this risk for you. As you look at your options and their cost you will be able to plan for a rainy day, so to speak. Some homes may have more risk than you are willing to take. If you know the area you are targeting to live in you will know what many of these risks are before you make an offer on a specific home.

You don't want a money pit; you are looking for a great investment. Here are some items to consider as you evaluate the home and area.

BUILDING CODE/ZONING COMPLIANCE: Check with zoning officials in the city or county, whichever is applicable, to verify the home passed inspections and has a current occupancy permit. Check to make sure your intended use of the property for business, rental, or residential use is permitted. If the basement was finished after the original final inspection did they get a permit to make the changes? If not, how does that affect you?

How many people, individuals or families, are allowed to live in the home? What uses are allowed? Has anything been built on the lot that the city does not know about? If so it could be a future problem for you.

RENTAL OF PROPERTY: Are you allowed to rent the home? Some properties do not allow rentals. Check with zoning officials and with local HOA to verify this use. Use may be subject to change and conditional use will have requirements. There could be a waiting list in developments that restrict how many units can be used as rentals.

HAZARDOUS WASTE AND TOXIC SUBSTANCES: You are probably thinking what would that be? Fuel tanks on the property, oil spilled on the property, methamphetamines, radon gas, lead and lead based paint, asbestos, and any illegal materials, to name some possibilities.

Real Estate Street Smarts

SURVEYING AND STAKING: Evaluate the property lines for accuracy. Mistakes can be made and they can affect you as the property owner. Land outside traditional subdivisions have greater chance of problems but even in a planned subdivision that has been through the building department you can have property boundary disputes. Remember it is a good idea to check with neighbors, the seller, and the governing officials, city or county, for potential problems. Have a survey done if there is a question.

HOME WARRANTY PLANS: Home warranties are insurance policies you can buy to warrant the working items of the home. The cost depends on the size of the home and how many pieces of equipment the home has, such as furnaces, water heaters, air conditioners, and toilets. The coverage is to repair or replace, at the company's choice, any item they cover for a one-year period. You can buy these for additional years at additional cost. Products are available for new construction and existing homes. Each time the company warrants a different item the consumer pays their deductible. These deductibles currently range from 50-100 dollars per trade item.

The upfront cost of the coverage starts at approximately $250 and goes up from there. It works like other insurance products, if you have a covered item break that costs more than the original cost of the warranty plus the deductible you save money. If nothing breaks you spent more on the warranty than you saved by having the warranty. Insurance is a way to spread your repair cost risk. You must read the terms of the insurance product to know what you are getting and you must call the insurance company before any work is done, in order to be covered. The warranty company decides who comes out to check the item and do the work needed.

There are requirements stated in the terms that make it possible for an item not to be covered. I have had clients that have had problems and clients that have been happy with the insurance. You will need to decide what is best for you. If you are a person that always gets the extended warranty on items you buy you will view this differently than those that never get the insurance. Look back at times you have or have not done this to evaluate if it has been a good choice or not. Also evaluate the condition of the items that will be covered by the policy to determine if repairs are likely in the time the policy is in effect.

Some Real Estate Purchase Contracts will have a home warranty spelled out in the contract. If one will be included, you need to know who will select it, who will pay for it, and how much it will cost.

FLOOD ZONE AND INSURANCE: Some homes will be in an area that is called a flood zone. There are different types of flood zones that are distinguished by the likelihood or risk of flooding categorized in years. A one-hundred year flood-zone is likely to flood every one hundred years as the estimated risk. A fifty-year flood zone has twice the risk.

Your lender may require flood insurance for the property you select. When you evaluate your home you should always evaluate which insurance riders, like flood or earthquake can be added and at what cost. This insurance can help you manage your risk of ownership and financial responsibility.

HOMEOWNERS INSURANCE: Check with insurance providers for availability of homeowners insurance, and the terms of the coverage. This coverage is also known as fire insurance. It can also perform other functions such as insuring your personal property to the amount agreed to in the policy. It can also include personal injury or other items. Your lender will require the insurance to loan you money on the house.

You will want to work with an insurance agent that will explain different options you have and help you understand their benefits and their cost to determine what coverage is best for you. They can help you decide on what riders you may want to add and what level of coverage to buy for your specific situation. Insurance companies track homes and people in their system. It is possible that a home or a person that has too many claims recorded would not be insurable. Check for coverage availability during your inspection period. This can be as simple as a phone call.

TITLE ISSUES/HOMEOWNER'S ASSOCIATION: Know what restrictions are recorded on the title. You will have to comply with these Covenants Conditions and Restrictions. Most home lots have easements for utility access and other uses. You are not allowed to build permanent structures on areas affected by the easement, such as pools, sheds, garages, gazebos, etc. Most lots will have five to ten feet around the outside edge of the property and some lots have other easements outside of the typical easements for the home and subdivision. Read your title report ,review the plat map, and check on all the restrictions and easements! If there is an HOA and/or CC&R's (Covenants Conditions and Restrictions) they are mentioned on the title report in connection with the property. The CC & R's tend to be long, but you need to know what you are agreeing to. Take the time to read them. Ask the title company about all the items on the report so you understand what each item is. The title report will have a phone number and contact name for you to direct any questions. Check the title during your inspection period to detect any judgments or other potential problems you or the seller could have when closing on the home. This will give you the opportunity to double check how much the seller has in loans on the property to make sure they can afford to sell the home. The seller could also have mechanics liens that will need to be addressed by the title company. Find and work on these items early to avoid delay and failure.

Real Estate Street Smarts

PHYSICAL CONDITION: Hire a home inspector to inspect and evaluate the home condition and possible liabilities for you. The few hundred you spend on this is well worth it unless you have the knowledge to do this for yourself. In addition to the inspector, you as the buyer should take the time to carefully look at the entire home to finalize your purchase decision. After you buy, it is yours for good and bad. You can limit your risk of loss by carefully evaluating the problems and potential future problems of the home. No home is perfect, every home will have items to take care of. You want to avoid homes that are too costly to maintain and repair. If it is not reoccurring problems, you may have the seller pay for what is needed to fix the problem or lower the price to compensate for the need.

Homes that have reoccurring problems could be so cost prohibitive that you end up being better off finding a new home, rather than dealing with a problem that cannot be resolved. Consider your total cost of ownership as you evaluate the home. An inspector can give you an idea of how old the equipment of the home is, and how long those items typically last. If you have a furnace that is twenty-five years old you should plan on replacing it in the near future, or you could even ask the seller if they would replace it for you. Most people forget to change the air filters on their furnace system. Changing the filter will save you money on utility cost and help the furnace last longer because it will not have to work as hard.

SQUARE FOOTAGE/ACREAGE: Pricing of the property is based on the size of the home and the land that is included in the sale. Just like you would count to see if you had all your items purchased at the store, you should check what you are buying when you buy real estate. An appraisal report will have the size of the home on it. Appraisers and the county recorder estimate the size as part of their work, you can check both as a reference. You can also hire a surveyor to check this for you, or you can get out a tape measure and do some math yourself to verify what has been advertised to you.

You don't need the size down to the exact foot, but you do want to know you are getting what you are paying for. It is possible for a seller to advertise a larger size than is actually there. Check your contract Tax ID number, or parcel number to double check the land, or parcels of land, that are included with the sale.

If the size is wrong, discuss and negotiate with the seller to resolve the problem. It could be an innocent mistake, or not. When you sell, your buyer will also want to get what they are paying for.

UTILITY SERVICES: Verify availability of all utility providers and systems. Check for any problems. Ask about deposit requirements. If the home has a private system, such as a septic tank instead of a city sewer hookup, have the system checked. Ask the seller for a copy of their utility bill, if possible, for winter and summer months, to help you get an idea how much your cost will be and how efficient the home is.

Ask utility providers if they know of any rebates available if you replace equipment in the home. Evaluate what the systems are powered by. Some homes will be gas, electric, propane, or a mixture of both.

WATER: Types of water include a private well, public well, culinary water (city drinking water), pressurized irrigation, secondary water, water rights, or water shares. Water quality and supply are a big deal for most people. Check out the water supply and system. You can add purifier systems to the home if you decide to, but know what you are starting with. Wells can have problems with water supply that may involve a well pump or the water level below ground changing. This could require drilling lower into the water source or even drilling a new well.

If you are buying water shares or rights verify with the appropriate water company to make sure they are attached to the property and can be accessed/used for the property, or that they can be transferred if they are coming from another property.

Watering with culinary drinking water is more expensive than other forms of gray, or dirty water such as irrigation water. Check what is available to you and take advantage of your options.

GEOLOGIC CONDITIONS: Have a geologist check the soil, the property, and the surroundings to discover potential concerns. At very least take the time to evaluate the situation for your self.

MOLD: Water, and wood in its many forms, with poor airflow cause mold. Water damage and health risks from mold can affect your use and enjoyment of the home. Be sure to check with appropriate professionals. Home inspectors can check for mold and you can get more information from the EPA at *www.epa.gov*

HOUSING COMPLIANCE: Real estate agents are required not to direct you to locations or homes with regard to race, color, religion, sex, national origin, marital status, age, handicap or familial status and any other requirements of federal and state fair housing laws.

You must be the one to decide what kind of neighborhood you want to live in. Check out the neighborhood or property conditions including, schools; proximity and adequacy of law enforcement; proximity to commercial, industrial, or agricultural activities; crime statistics; fire protection; other governmental services; existing and proposed transportation; construction and development; noise or odor from any source; and other nuisances, hazards, or circumstances.

PROPERTY TAXES: You can find this information on your title report. Verify the annual amount. Once a year you can contest the valuation if you have reason to believe it is too high. By providing sold reports of similar homes you may be able to reduce your taxes. In your notice from the county they inform you of your ability to dispute the assessment.

Remember as home prices go up so will your taxes and as a result your housing costs.

INCOME TAX/LEGAL CONSEQUENCES: The government changes the tax code frequently. Your accountant or CPA (Certified Public Accountant) will be able to tell you, with your situation, how buying and owning the property will affect you. Many people sell homes without having taxes due. You may have taxes due from the sale. Talk to your advisors before you buy or sell any property.   Your attorney will be able to explain legal consequences regarding the property and the contracts associated with it.

Conclusion: It is best to have a professional help you in each of these categories. If your budget will not allow for professionals in each category to help you, don't skip it. Do some research on your own and do the best you can, use what you know and your own common sense. It is better than closing your eyes and hoping for the best.

To find resources and contact information for professionals that can help you visit our website at *www.RESmartMoves.com*

When problems come up, don't blow them out of proportion. All homes, even new homes have some things that need to be improved. Many of the items on a home inspectors list will serve as education and as a maintenance list for you. These items are not a big deal but do deserve attention. Ask the seller to take care of them but don't start your search over because you need to change 5 electrical outlets and add drain spout extenders to the home. Many things on inspection reports are not a big deal. You can talk with you home inspector about the difference between major items of concern and minor ones.

-Chapter 11-
Negotiation, What Sellers Need To Know.

As the seller, you want to get the best possible contract for your home. You want a contract that is likely to close. You want to avoid risky contracts that jeopardize all your plans, and put your money at risk.

As the seller, you will want to evaluate the buyers situation at the beginning of your contract negotiations. Find out what things they want and what they actually need. Look for things that you can do for them, that they value, that are not a problem for you as the seller.

As you negotiate talk about terms and money not personal items. You must not say or do anything that would put you in violation of Federal Fair Housing Law. You cannot discriminate based on Race, Color, Religion, Sex, National Origin, Marital Status, Age, Handicap, or Familial Status. In Utah it also includes Source of Income.

It is business not personal. Personal items should not be involved in the negotiations. If they are qualified and are willing to pay an acceptable price with acceptable terms, that is all you need to know.

You need to do your homework on the buyers ability to qualify for a loan before you tie up your house. A buyer that does not have a good chance of successfully closing is actually worse than no buyer at all. The only time this is not true is when you use a bad offer to entice other good buyers to make an offer on your property.

Before you negotiate an accepted contract, find out if the buyer has a home to sell. Even if they do not make their offer subject to the sale of a home, they could have one they have to sell. You need to know this up front. The buyer is not required to tell you unless you ask, so ASK!!!

Buyers may be willing to risk earnest money, but that is not what you want as a seller, you want the home sold. Making plans, preparing to move and having it all fall apart on you is not any fun. This can happen at any point up until it is recorded at the county recorders office. Only then are you truly done.

If the buyer does have a home to sell and wants to buy your home anyway, you will need to check with their lender to make sure they qualify with both homes and make sure the lender is well aware of their plan. If they say they will close before they sell the other home you should only give them 30 to 45 days to close, or ask for increased non-refundable earnest money.

Require all offers to have a lender letter with them. The lender letter needs to spell out the price they are approved for. Any conditions listed need to be evaluated to have the logical expectation that they are a good candidate for the loan. If the price on the lender letter and the offer price are close to the same you will want to talk to the lender or have your agent let the lender know you are concerned about the price being so close to their limit. Find out from the lender if this is a comfortable range for the buyer. Can they actually qualify for more than this, but they don't want to spend more, or are they really pushing the limit?

Understand that a buyer that is at the max of their qualifications is risky. It will not take much to change, even during escrow, with spending or wages to cross the line and not meet the requirements for the loan.

You can also ask the lender if they are comfortable with the dates on the contract. And have they talked to the buyer about not applying for other credit prior to closing, such as: the purchase of a truck, car, big screen TV, furniture etc..

The purpose of the call is not to dig for personal details that the lender can't answer because of privacy issues, but to ask general questions that will help you know what type of borrower you are dealing with. They may volunteer details such as FICO scores if the buyer allows it. You can, by including it in the contract, have the buyer meet with your lender to show evidence of qualification, or you can have them agree to provide the details you want to discern their ability to close.

FOOD FOR THOUGHT

Sellers should be careful not to have the earnest money amount too high. If the seller defaults on the contract, not selling the home to the buyer for whatever reason, they are required to give the buyer the same amount of earnest money for damages. The buyer can refuse the earnest money and seek a different solution legally. Don't agree to more earnest money than you are willing to pay them if you are in default. One-half of one percent to one percent of the purchase price should be agreeable for both parties.

It is not hard to get a lender letter. It is a good start but you will want more information. Is the buyer pre-approved or approved? Realize when you talk to a lender they are working for the buyer so they are not likely to put their client in a bad light. If you know what to ask and have permission to get the information via your contract they will not be able to put a spin on reality.

If an offer comes in without a lender letter require a lender letter within 3 business days on a counteroffer. If they fail to provide the letter to the seller the seller may cancel the contract. This needs to be spelled out in your counteroffer. This way you get what you need or you have a way out. You don't want your house off the market unless it is likely to close. Word the counteroffer to spell out what will happen if they do not provide the lender letter within the time specified. Details always. You don't want a contract that is not clear or not easily followed.

The contract deadlines from the last chapter are great for most seller situations. The shorter the dates that you have to wait to find out if your buyer is going to work out for you, the better. You will be able to negotiate contracts that favor your wants and needs more when it is a sellers market and you will have to settle for the best you can get in a buyers market. Having high earnest money amounts and having a reasonable time for them to get approved for the loan will help you.

Anything that you want to happen for sure must be in writing and part of the contract. You must follow the contract exactly. Don't forget that sellers can be in default on the contract just as the buyer can. The seller has the first deadline of the contract to get disclosures on the property to the buyer. You should have the title work done before you have an offer so you can have the title company search the buyers names, add them to the report and get it to the buyer quickly. You should

> ### FOOD FOR THOUGHT
>
> **Don't spend the money until your transaction is totally and absolutely done, recorded and you have the money in hand!**

have the property disclosure form filled out and ready to go. All the disclosures must be delivered to the buyer. Get a receipt of delivery signed and dated showing your compliance with the contract.

Before you agree to a price you need to know your estimated costs to sell and know what items recorded on the title must be paid to sell the home. Any loans on the property, mechanics liens, or judgments must be paid or resolved to sell the home. You want to know before you sign a contract what you must pay off. If you don't, and find a surprise it can cost you. Most contracts give the buyer and seller the option to take the earnest money amount or to refuse the money and go the legal route in court to solve the problem. You could end up in court if you sign a contract to sell your home and end up in default because you can't or won't sell your home to the buyer.

Find out the timing situation of the buyer. When do they need to move in, and can they be flexible? You will do well to negotiate 72 hours of possession after the home closes to finish getting out. That way you know it will not fall through on you before you load your piano, furniture, and boxes into the truck.

If the buyers situation is flexible, make it the best case scenario for you. If they are in a situation with fixed dates that are hard to change and you can be flexible, do it. It would be better to give them the possession day the buyer needs but require them to close a few days earlier to give you the security you need. If buyers have an issue with the cost of the time prior to possession, offer to pay them for the 2 or 3 days. The more they get what they want, that does not negatively affect you, the better.

As the seller, be realistic on price. Look at what the buyer can buy if they don't buy your home. It is possible that the buyer will make you an offer but is not committed to pay whatever you ask. When the buyer looks at the sold, under contract, and active comparisons they will come up with an estimated value. It may not be as high as your listed price. Their first offer will not likely be their highest offer either.

When negotiating price, leave emotion out of the picture. Your home is worth more to you because of the memories you have in the home and the bond you have with the home. Buyers do not have this same feeling. If a home that is similar is offered for less, they will happily pay less for what would be, to them, the same thing.

The value of the home will differ from buyer to buyer. Generally they will have the same price range based on market information but some will be low and some higher and some in between. The buyer knows the active competition, the seller should too. The seller's knowledge of the market will help them know when they are likely getting the highest price possible from the buyer.

If you have a low offer that is not even in the range of reality, reply with a reality check for them at an appropriate price and then let it go. If they are serious they will come back. If not you will have moved on to a serious buyer. The market changes so pay close attention.

Learn from buyer's feedback and offers. It is possible that you are evaluating the property high because of your feelings for the home. If you receive multiple offers and they are all below your acceptable price range you should seriously reevaluate your price.

The first one to speak, loses. If you feel the buyer really wants the home but they are just negotiating hard with you, try staying firm and giving them some time to think about the house. The home must be worth it to you if it will be worth it to them. If you have priced the home well, meaning at a price a smart buyer would pay and an appraisal will support, it is smart to stay firm on your price.

If you are firm, the buyer will know they are getting the best deal on the home. That will help them from second-guessing themselves by thinking we should have offered lower, we are paying too much. This is why even with flexible sellers it is a good idea to counteroffer and not take the first price the buyer suggests. The counteroffer will help the buyer realize that they would not have done better if they offered lower.

Remember buyers don't start with their best price unless they are competing with other buyers. Final offers can be powerful if you indeed mean what you say. If you want a certain price, and you will not go under that amount, tell the buyer. The buyer wants to know they are getting the best deal possible. It is a yes or no proposition. You will not likely start with this unless you are firm on your listed price.

As a seller you should make your offer to the buyer appealing by not changing the structure of the buyers offer, when possible. If they have asked you to pay closing costs for them and it will not cause a problem with an appraisal, simply raise the price and leave the closing costs in the offer. If the appraisal could be a problem, find out if the buyer has the funds to pay the closing costs if they had to, and then offer to include the closing costs if the appraisal comes in at the purchase price. Specify that the buyer would pay the closing costs above the appraised amount if the home appraises for less.

The goal is to have a transaction that can close. If the buyer cannot pay their closing costs, you will be risking a little time to see if the home will appraise at their amount. In this situation you will want the deadline for the appraisal to be as short as possible, about ten to fourteen days is very fair to the buyer and to you as the seller.

The more demand that is perceived by the buyer, who offers on your home, the more money you will get for the home. You should look to create multiple offer situations. If you hear someone is sending you an offer or you get an offer in, no matter if the offer is any good, you should tell all the recent showings, (buyers who have been through the home recently) that you have an offer on the home and that you are calling to let them know. If they have any interest in the home please make an offer before a certain date and time. This time should be before your response deadline on the offer you have.

This will motivate all buyers who are serious about your home. You should be fair with all buyers. If you decide to go with an open bid, you should be open and tell everyone the highest bid amount. If you go with a silent bid, treat each offer the same by not telling anyone what the offer details are. You can talk with your agent to get options that you can consider, in multiple offer situations.

If your home has only been on the market for a few days consider taking offers for one week, then negotiating after the week. This way you will get an accurate idea of the demand for the property. If you have an offer that quickly you must have a good price.

Most buyers and sellers are not in the business of negotiations. They are likely to lose interest in the other party after the third and fourth counteroffer. At that point they usually don't feel there is common ground for the two parties.

Look for solutions when you negotiate. Is there another way you can give the buyer what they want or accomplish what they are trying to do? Can a two thousand dollar concern about an old furnace be satisfied by paying less than 400 dollars for a home warranty? Maybe: it is definitely worth a try. Look for ways to make it work, legally of course, instead of reasons it won't work.

If you have any direct contact with the buyer you can personalize the transaction. This works both ways of course and you may be affected more than the buyer is by knowing who they are. Both the buyer and the seller should be careful what they say around the other party. If you tell them a figure that is lower than you are willing to go or imply that you are flexible when you are firm they will not be able to get that out of their mind.

Look at included items as a great opportunity to provide value for the buyer. The seller is usually in a better position to replace appliances if necessary. You may be able to get more out of your home by including a refrigerator, range, microwave, washer, and dryer. You could even include another item that is less basic like a pool table, TV, or a hot tub.

The value for the buyer is the ability to have these items worked into the deal and the loan. The buyer may not have the cash on hand to replace all the items they need. The seller will likely have cash available from the sale of the home.

Everyone likes to win a little. If you do not budge on any term of the contract the buyer will likely have hard feelings about it. Give them what you can but stay on track with your goals for the sale. There are many terms in the contract. Surely they want something that you can give them, keeping in mind that a little can go a long way.

When you negotiate the only thing you risk is the loss of the buyer. If this is the only buyer that will be interested in your home, you priced it too high.

Realize that until the home is sold, recorded, and totally done, the buyer could be trying to negotiate with you. There are many times that requests may come in. During inspections, ap-

FOOD FOR THOUGHT

If, as a seller, you have an appraisal problem, evaluate the appraisal the buyer has had done. If it does not look fair and accurate to you, order a second opinion from another appraiser. The $400 spent on the second opinion can and has saved thousands of dollars for sellers. Don't just roll over, get a second opinion if you feel it is probable to increase the appraised value. If the second opinion is like the first drop your price to get the deal done. Another buyer will not want to pay more than appraised value for your home. It is not likely that you will find a buyer that wants to pay, in cash, above the amount of appraisal. The lender will not be willing, and few homes are purchased without a loan.

praisal, loan denial, and the final walk through. The buyer at any given time may be using negotiating tactics to get you down even more. Think through and consider professional advice when you receive requests. Saying no can be the right answer, but it isn't always.

In a buyers market you may need to be very aggressive to capture and keep your buyer. In these markets the seller with the buyer is the winner.

You can keep a buyer after a home inspection that does not go well, by taking care of items for the buyer to help them not feel overwhelmed and overextended financially. Many times these items are not expensive but can feel more challenging to the buyer than they need to be.

If you meet your goals for the sale of your home and the home closes, you have successfully negotiated your contract. It is not over until it is over. You should only be surprised if you have no surprises.

Real Estate Street Smarts

-Chapter 12-
Prepare Your Home To SELL

Just like you would detail your car before you sell it, you will do better selling when you have prepared your home. A buyer's first impression of your home will be the only impression they have. Inside and out you have one shot at a buyer.

Both the inside and outside of the home are important. The first thing buyers will see is the outside of the home. Many buyers drive by the home to see the outside and the neighborhood before they make an appointment to see the inside. If the outside is not up to par you will miss out on some buyers. The more buyers you get into your house the more chances you have to sell your home.

The outside of your home should be well kept. The landscaping should be neat and not overgrown. Flowers and other trees or plants will provide depth and color to the landscape of your yard.

Weeds, dead grass and other unsightly and seemingly unkempt areas will distract and discourage buyers. They will assume the home has not been cared for.

Walkways and entrances need to be clear of branches from trees or bushes. No one should be ducking around branches to get into your home. Trimming trees, bushes, and grass will send the right signals to the buyer that your home has been well maintained.

If you have fencing or a deck, it should be in good repair and should have a fresh coat of stain. If your wood improvements need stain, the buyer will be thinking about how much work it will be and how often they will have to stain them. You want them thinking about how nice it looks and how much they benefit from having the deck or the fenced yard.

Keep your yard, even your back yard, neat. Pick up yard toys and make sure walk areas are clear for the buyer as they come through any access from the home into the yard.

The outside of your home is important to a buyer. Outside items of your home are perceived to be expensive to change. The outside of the home is the only part of the home most of the public will see. If it looks rundown you will only attract deal hunters. An average buyer wants a home that will look good, something they can be proud of and not embarrassed by.

A new coat of paint on all exterior doors and door trim is a must. They do not look good when they are weathered and flaking. The front door makes an impression on the buyer. The door should be in good working order and looking good. The lock and doorknob should also look good and work easily. If you have a door that sticks, adjust it. If it squeaks lubricate the hinges.

Wash the outside of your home including the windows. If you have any trim that needs repair or paint, do the maintenance. If you have shingles that are missing or damaged, fix them. If the whole roof is terrible, look at replacing it. Replace any broken window panes and make sure all windows open and lock.

If you have concrete that has settled, look into concrete lifting services. They pump a mixture under the concrete and lift it back into place. If you have concrete with an unsightly surface, look into resurfacing or replacing it.

Your goal with your work on your home inside and out is to make it look great and spend as little as possible. Driveways can be resurfaced at a lower cost than replacement. Sinks, tubs and even countertops can be resurfaced at a lower cost than replacement.

If you have a pet consider this: Some buyers have pets and some don't. Some people have allergies. Buyers can have strong feelings when it comes to pets inside or outside. Buyers who love pets will not be bothered by a home that does not have a pet, but your pet may bother buyers who do not have pets.

If you want as many buyers as possible, get rid of the signs of a pet. Fix any damage inside and out and find a friend or family member to board and take care of your pet while you are selling. If having your pet out of the house is not an option, do a great job cleaning up after them and take them out for all showings.

On the inside of your home you want the buyer thinking how clean and nice your home is. Trust me, if you do your work here, you will stand out. You would be surprised how many people do not prepare their home to sell it. Your home will have an advantage because it will show much better than other homes that you are competing against.

Buyers often make buying decisions on the feel of the home. You will help them with this feeling by making your house "their new house". As buyers walk through the home, you want them thinking about how the house will work for them. You want them to see it as their house and not your house.

Remove things that will distract a buyer. Take down your family history picture wall. You don't have to reinvent the wheel here. If you have ever been in a model home they decorate with beautiful but not personal items. Scenic pictures and many other different types of art should replace the family picture wall.

Your goal should be to keep the buyer thinking about themselves and not about what hairstyle you had when you got married. For security and safety do not have the names of your children on the walls in their bedrooms or in any other place in the home. These are strangers that will be in your home after all. Plus we want them thinking about their own kids and not yours.

Every home that people actually live in has nicks and dings in the walls and scuffmarks on moldings. It is normal, but it is not how you want your home when you sell. Deep clean your home. We are talking about the white glove test, every nook and cranny should be cleaned. Patch and paint any walls that do not look great. Use colors that people will like. Now is not the time to scream personality through loud paint colors. Even décor can be distracting if it is too extreme.

The baseboards, door trim, doors, and other moldings will need a new coat of paint. This will make a huge difference in the appeal of the home. You want your home looking new. Cabinets can be cleaned and touched up. If necessary, the wood can be refinished.

Carpets should be cleaned. If you have floors or other items that are damaged, repair or replace them. They need to look good when you are done. If they do not the buyer will automatically reduce the value of your home in their mind because of the cost they will have in replacing the item.

You can get items fixed or replaced for less than most buyers will estimate it will cost them. If you do not take care of an item you will end up paying for it twice. First with the impression it leaves with buyers and second with an allowance or reduction in price so the buyer can take care of it. **Don't underestimate the value of your home showing like new.**

Areas that are unfinished should be neatly swept and free of spider webs and clutter. These areas should be organized and work well for their intended purpose. You will want the garage to look as big as possible. Keep cars in it while your home is for sale. This may mean you need a storage unit for items you have in the garage. If you have a storage room put items from the garage there.

Furniture placement is important. You will want good flow through the home as buyers walk through. Do not have narrow areas because of furniture placement. You want to create an open feel. Areas that feel constricted will not impress buyers. Rooms should be decorated for their intended use or multiple uses of the room.

How your furniture is arranged and how much furniture you have in a room changes the feel of the room. You want the furniture to add to the value of the room and not attract the buyer's attention to the furniture itself. If you have furniture in bad condition consider removing it if possible, or consider using a cover to improve the appearance.

It is your opportunity to show buyers the great possibilities with each room of your home. Try moving furniture around a few different ways to see what is best for each room. You will surprise yourself. You may even like it.

All the items in your home should be working. If you have cover plates on outlets that are cracked replace them. If your disposal or anything else does not work, fix or replace it. You want everything working well and looking good. Make sure all light bulbs are working. This will make your home light and bright. Your home will show better with the lights on, even in the day. All this work will help you sell your house and will also help you get through your buyer inspections after you have a signed contract. It takes effort, but you will be very glad you took the time and a little money to make this happen.

There will be things in your home that are not ideal. These items can be, what we call, a deal killer for a buyer. Be creative in ways you can remedy problems you see before you put your home on the market, and after as you learn more about your home from potential buyers as they come through.

Always ask for feedback from the buyers that come through your home. Ask them what they like and what they don't like. How does it compare to other homes they have seen.

You only need one buyer. If a common problem for a buyer is something that is not easily remedied consider embracing it. Think about which buyers would like it the way it is, and do everything you can to make your home appealing to them. If you have 2 bedrooms together and you keep receiving feedback about buyers wanting 3 or more bedrooms together try to make your home more appealing to empty nesters, singles or newly married buyers.

Always look for solutions to improve your situation. Listen carefully to the suggestions from your professional help. Keep your home cleaned and maintained while you are selling. This is more work than you would normally do if you were just living in the home, but you are not just living, you are selling.

Packing up your personal and extra items should not be a problem because you _are_ moving.

Security.

Take some thought before you have strangers in your home about what you have in plain sight. It is not common to have a security problem while selling, but it can happen.

People who are addicted to drugs get very creative to get their fix. Prescription drugs have become popular for users. They also will steal items they can sell to buy the drugs they want. You should put any drugs you have in the home out of site and in a place they would not expect to find them. Don't keep them in your medicine cabinet.

Anything that has great value to you sentimentally, or otherwise should be packed up and put in a safe place. You do not want these items in plain site or even in a drawer that is easily accessible. Don't leave your keys to cars and other items hanging on a hook in plain site. Take them with you or put them in a safe place.

Drawers can get opened, but placing your things in a drawer is better than leaving them out in the open. Do not leave anything of great importance in a place that they can wander off, if you know what I mean.

For the safety of your family and real estate professionals as well, do not keep any weapons in plain site or in places they could be easily used. Guns, knives, swords, and weapons of any kind should be kept in a safe place. This includes the kitchen knives that are likely sitting in a block on your kitchen counter. These should be put out of site. Providing a weapon to a person that would harm another is not a good idea. You will need these knives to use each day so find a place that will work like behind something in your pantry out of site for example. This way you will know where they are but a stranger will not. You will only need to keep them there when you are having showings.

When you have a professional help you with buyers seeing your home, they can talk to you about keybox options that can be used to keep your home secure and restrict the viewers to those authorized to be in your home. An agent can control access to the home by using a keybox that only allows members of the board of realtors to access the key in the box. These keybox systems can also have lockout times during the night. The box will not open in the middle of the night even for the owner of the box. It also helps you know who has been in the home.

If you do not like the idea of having a keybox on your home consider having a keybox, but not permanently attaching it so you can take it inside when you do not have showing appointments and setting it out on the porch when you do. This can be a great solution for everyone. When agents and buyers have a legitimate appointment they can easily access the home and you as the seller control when people are in your home. No morning surprises while you are having a late shower. It is through experience that I know that the communication of a showing does not always make it to any or all of the residence of the home for sale. It happens more often than I would like.

In most cases it is better for the homeowner to be gone when a buyer is shown the home. This allows for the buyer to speak freely and visualize the home as their own and not the current owners, and this makes the buyer feel much more comfortable in the home. If you are home when a buyer comes and you are leaving for the showing, lock the door and have them use the keybox to make sure they have authorized access to the home. Your agent can look up the agent on their MLS system to verify they are licensed and a board member. It also allows appraiser and home inspectors access if they are members of the board of realtors.

If you are selling on your own someone will need to be home when buyers are looking at the house. Try to have another adult around or make a phone call to a friend so they know you are home and people are there to see the house. It is a good idea for your personal safety.

Real Estate Street Smarts

You may think this is over-the-top, but it is better to plan for what could happen than to have it happen and wish you had done things differently. As with everything in this book this is not intended as a complete list of every possible thing that could happen, but is intended to give you basics to start from and get you thinking so you can take full advantage of your own knowledge and the experience of the professionals that help you.

-Chapter 13-
Protect Yourself From Scams And Fraud

We do not want you, or anyone for that matter, to be a victim of fraud or get scammed during your real estate adventure. Honesty is a wonderful thing. Think of how many problems we would not have if everyone was completely honest with everyone they had contact with.

People who decide they want to make money dishonestly are hard workers and could also be described as being smart or creative. We will not be able to give you a list of every possible thing to watch out for. It is not possible, new scams will always be created. What you will learn is important concepts and hopefully you will have the motivation to verify what people tell you.

I will give you some examples to get the point across. All of them come down to something as simple as a lie. These are some of my personal favorites.

Loan fraud is simple and yet complicated. It is simple because if you mislead or misrepresent yourself, the terms of the purchase, or your relationship in the transaction, you are in violation of federal law. This results in fines and possible jail time for those involved.

It is complicated because there are many intricate and seemingly innocent scams that are almost logical. After all, an attorney or another professional said it was all "above board". Just remember when someone tells you something that sounds too good to be true, it most likely is too good to be true, and professionals have been known to be put in jail from lying to good people like you. Being a professional does not make you honest.

A very well-known agent working with high-end homes in Utah County was convicted. Realtors, an appraiser, an investor, a title company and an escrow officer were all involved in the fraud. In their scam they pushed up values to very high, false levels, took loans out on these properties with false appraisals and fake buyers, getting rich off the lenders money. They mislead some buyers, telling them they did not need to pay the mortgage, and the lenders were left holding the bag. This agent threw away a great business and totally devastated his family. It was not expected by anyone.

The agent reported sold home information incorrectly on the MLS to get higher appraisals in the future. You can learn from this that if a home sold for much more than all the other homes you are comparing to determine the value of your home, you should ask questions. Call the agents involved to get details of the sale to find out why it is so different than other sold information you have. You likely will find out why there is a difference. If there is not a good reason, you will want to remove it from your comparison completely.

Another type of loan fraud is the use of double contracts. The buyer and seller will have a contract to sell the home at a higher price than originally agreed, the buyer will get a loan based on the higher amount, then the buyer and seller will split the extra amount to put cash in their pocket. In some cases a company is formed for the buyer and the seller to justify the legitimacy of the transaction.

The reality is this: The price the buyer is willing to pay is the price minus the cash that the seller and buyer receive above the original price. The only reason the buyer is willing to have the price higher is because they are getting cash from it.

Buyers use this concept to eliminate their down payment. They usually do this by having the seller give them a fake second loan for the down payment that the buyer and seller know will not ever be paid. In this way, they trick the lender into lending 100% or more of the purchase when the bank thinks they are lending 90% of the value of the home giving them a 10% cushion if the buyer defaults on the loan. But what they really have is a loan over 100%. The reality is they have no cushion. Who is hurt if the buyer does not pay the mortgage? The buyers credit is trashed, but that may be worth $100,000 cash. The seller does not care because they received more money for the home. The BANK is the one who is left with all the real pain. Or if you want to think about that one step further, it is all of us that apply for honest loans that get to pay higher cost to offset losses the company takes on. Businesses are in business to make money, and if they don't they are out of business. Only the government can print more money.

Providing false borrower information to qualify for a loan seems obviously wrong, but it happens all too much. The borrower, agent, or the lender falsifies documentation of income or tax returns, even social security numbers and other personal information to qualify for the loan. It is all a lie, and the bank is left holding the bag with a buyer who should not have received a loan and may have never planned to make a payment on the home. They instead just plan on living in the home for four months to a year or more for free until the home is foreclosed on.

So the borrower, that may already have bad credit, gets to enjoy some free housing while the loan officer enjoys the money they have been paid to originate the loan, or an agent enjoying the commission, and the bank just gets to lose money.

It does make you think that perhaps loans should be kept by the originator for one to two years before they could be sold. That way the lenders making these loans would have a horse in the race. Now we have lenders that sell these loans immediately and don't carry any risk from originating a bad loan.

Using another persons credit for a fee was very popular when stated income loans were available. Builders/Investors would pay a substantial fee to a person who would let them use their credit and qualification to get a loan for a home to be built. The person receiving the fee has nothing to do with the home and never intended to buy it, live in it or be involved at all with the property.

The builder/investor builds the home with the borrowed money with plans to sell the home. All they care about is getting a person with a high credit score to sign, building the house and selling it for a large profit. It does not matter to the builder what the income level of the person really is. They are just going to sell the home to someone else. If the home does not sell, they may let it go to the bank.

The person that collected the fee could have their credit damaged severely, but the builder has little money in the property to lose and has no risk to his own credit standing. The builder also receives money to build the house from the construction loan. It is the bank that has most, if not all, the actual money loss. You can bet that the bank would not be okay with the loan if they really knew what was happening. They would not lend the money if they knew the person on the loan did not have any attachment to the home. In the post credit crisis lending market banks will be more careful who they lend money to.

Flipping homes without adding value. This is when investors buy a home at market value then immediately sell it for a profit without increasing the value of the home by improving the property. The value of the home has not changed. Investors will build up false demand, sold comparisons, and appraisals by buying homes from themselves in a different company name, or from other investors, thus pushing the values up falsely. They build it up in an area then after raising the values they sell to an unknown party and disappear with their incredible profit. The innocent buyer of the home finds out when they go to sell that others are not interested at the price they paid for the home. Banks look for homes that have been sold multiple times in a short period of time--since the bank is the other victim of these scams.

Investors, who say they will save homeowners that are facing foreclosure, but don't. There are many inventive ways people scam others that find themselves in a tight spot financially with their home. In this scam the investor usually tells the at risk homeowner that they will fix their problem. The investor tells the homeowner that they just need to sign over the house, and he will pay the back interest and any fees to get the loan current. They will then rent the home to the homeowner and then the homeowner will be able to buy it back to keep from losing their home. The problem is all in the lie. The investor does not pay a dime to the lender. They do take the rent money from the homeowner and pocket it. They enrich themselves until the bank takes the home through foreclosure. The homeowner's hope of keeping the home vanishes along with all the money they paid the scam artist.

Many times the homeowner is in a situation that will not work for renting the home. The investor tells the homeowner that he will save their credit so they can buy a home again very soon. This is done by paying the loan current and getting new renters in to pay the mortgage.

The homeowner moves out, and renters move in. The renters pay the investor a deposit, and each month pay rent for three or four months until the bank takes the house. None of this money goes to the lender but all into the investor's pocket. The investor disappears. The legitimate renters are kicked out and lose their deposit because the investor cannot be found. The homeowner gets a foreclosure on their credit.

The laws are different depending on the state your home is located in, but in Utah the bank can file a notice of default after you miss one payment. The homeowner is likely 30 days late or more on their mortgage when the notice is filed. The law gives the homeowner 90 days from the notice to bring the loan current and keep their home. Half of notice of defaults are brought current and not foreclosed on by the bank. As you can see there are at very least four months the homeowner can live in the home without making any payments. In some states the foreclosure process takes much longer. Because of these laws, the homeowner could have lived in the home for four months at no cost to get back on their feet but instead are only left with the foreclosure they were trying to avoid in the first place.

There are transactions of legitimate investors that do similar programs honestly. The key word here is honestly. When you sell creatively like this with an honest investor you need to manage your risk. You are still on the loan. It is smart to have the new buyer/renter make payments to you or an escrow company and you then give the money to the bank. If they don't give you the monthly payments you know the bank isn't getting the money and you can do something about it. You may even decide that renting your home out and trying to work out a plan with your lender works better anyway. Talking with your lender and other professionals to get advice when you are in a tough situation is critical.

Bad loan modification companies. These companies are advertised as people who help borrowers get their home loans modified. They prey on people in a tight spot that need a modification to keep their home. In desperation they pay the company an up front fee for the help of the company to get the loan modified.

The companies offering this are a scam in my book, because of two things. Many times when the fee is charged up front it is because the company knows the service they provide you is no good. They are not willing to gamble payment on their results, and you shouldn't either. Second you can and should contact your lender directly to let them know of your difficulty and get the paperwork started for the lender to decide if they will modify your loan.

Understand that lenders do not want to modify your loan if they can avoid it. In some situations modifying would save the lender money in my view. Banks lose money when they take a home in foreclosure or through a short sale.

Don't pay an upfront fee to have help modifying your loan. Lenders and legitimate groups offer this help for free.

What you should do. Verify what people tell you. Get more than one opinion. Don't let people hard sell you in their pushy way. If you must act now there is a reason, and that is that if you think about it or research it you will figure out that you don't want to do it. That is why they pressure you to act quickly. Reputable people will give you time to think about any offer they have for you.

You should get offers and other details in writing. If it is not in writing you have nothing. People, including professionals, may lie to you, telling you what they think you want to hear, knowing that it is not accurate. There are so many ways this is done. If they bait you in and switch on you, it is a scam, and you can put a stop to it.

Verify what you are told. Evaluate information for yourself to protect your own best interests. If it sounds too good to be true it probably is not true.

When a loan is involved be honest about the details of the transaction with the lender. Do not hide anything or try to get creative to find ways to get them to give you what you want. Do not do anything under the table. Everything needs to be on your settlement statement you sign at the title company. There should only be one settlement statement used for the transaction. It is okay to be creative if you are being honest with all the parties involved.

Life is better when we are honest with each other. Sadly, my home state of Utah has far too much room for improvement when it comes to fraud and scams. Utah has ranked number one for loan fraud in the past and has often been ranked in the top ten. Ranking number one is not an honor. The people of Utah need to do better. The entire country should do better. We can make a difference by being honest in our activities, and by knowing what to look out for we can avoid deals with dishonest people making the soil unfertile for these fraudsters and scammers. These dishonest people will go to more fruitful areas if "business" becomes hard for them.

Remember what these liars believe, "there is a sucker born everyday". Lets prove them wrong. Don't let it happen to you, and then share your knowledge with others to help keep them from a disaster.

Real Estate Street Smarts

Honesty needs to make a comeback! All of the United States can and should improve. Fraud affects all of us. We all pay more because of the dishonest people among us. We will pay less if honesty prevails in popular culture.

We should all stand up for honesty and correct principles. It really will make the world a better place.

Real Estate Street Smarts

-Chapter 14-
Maximize The Free Help Of A SMART MOVES Consumer Advocate.

We, at Smart Moves, want the world to be a better place. Wouldn't it be great if everyone would do the right thing? It would be ideal if others would look after your interests as if they were their own. That is not reality, but maybe with some work we can get a lot closer.

We feel that the best place to start is with you, the consumer. If we can empower you with knowledge, provide you with the tools you need, and the independent data needed to evaluate your situation, you can determine what direction will be best for your housing needs.

Consulting with a consumer advocate that is motivated by your well being and not a specific sale, is a great advantage. An advocate that will tell you when you are better off financially if you rent. When it is better for you to be content with your current housing, or to confirm that you are ready and it is a good time to buy if you want to. We will tell you what part of the real estate cycle you are in and how your timing affects your investment. We will tell you when it would be better to wait to sell. Not simply encouraging you to move forward, emphasizing reasons to sell, and not bringing up all the reasons not to sell as skilled salespeople often do.

We can't expect a salesperson to tell us we should not buy what they have to sell. It goes against human nature and reality. A salesperson, who is paid based on what they sell, must sell to survive. In fact, if you walked into a car dealer and they told you that now is not the right time for you to buy a car or that you can't afford it you would likely be offended or angry with them. We expect them to sell us a car.

Real estate is not like a car. The decisions you make about housing have a much larger impact on your quality of life. It is one area that we all want to go well. We don't want a lemon. We don't want you to get a lemon. There are tons of lemons out there. Because of the complexity and the details involved in real estate transactions there are many things that can become your own personal lemon.

Transactions will not be perfect but they can be much better, and they definitely can be designed with your own personal plan in mind. Avoiding train wrecks

---

FOOD FOR THOUGHT

> **You could be buying a great advantage for your future or you could be buying a devastating disaster that will leave a mark in your life that will be hard to forget.**

is half the battle. Real estate is not like any other purchase decision you make. Consumer Advocates help you plan your housing. You may remember the saying: <u>If you fail to plan you plan to fail</u>.

You benefit from consulting with us before selecting a salesperson to work with. By evaluating your situation and making and following your plans you stay in control. We put you in the driver's seat.

<u>Better planning will bring you better results</u>. You will know what is best for you because you have researched it and made your plans, both buying and selling. If you have ever had a salesperson tell you what you want instead of listening to what you want, you will appreciate the control you have when you are prepared and able to tell your salesperson what they can do for you.

Having help from professionals with the experience, knowledge, and contacts for the specific type of property you are dealing with, will make all the difference. Wouldn't it be great if you could know what you are getting before you hire someone? Here is the thing, you can! A consumer advocate can talk with you to find out what specific property type and area you are looking to sell or buy. We can give you the actual statistics of the best performing agents for the property type and location. This information is not what they tell you they do, while sitting with you in your living room, but is the actual data from the MLS system that records their transactions.

This data includes what homes they have sold recently. How long the properties were on the market. Did they lower the price from the original price. How many do they have contracts on right now. How many active homes do they have to sell. How many homes have they tried to sell but did not.

FOOD FOR THOUGHT

An experienced specialist will charge a similar, if not the same amount, as a new inexperienced agent or an agent that usually works with another type of real estate. You don't always get what you pay for.

A consumer advocate can help you evaluate your real estate professional options, provide education, answer questions, and set up interviews for you to meet the agents you feel are your best options. You decide who is best for you. If you do not like any of them, we look at other options. There are many companies and thousands of agents to choose from.

You don't have to be in the dark on this. We can shed some light on the situation for you. You can hire someone that specializes in what you have or want and has proven to be good at what they do.

Take advantage of this, **no cost**, consulting and referral service. The professional you choose pays a small portion of their commission to Smart Moves Consumer Advocates in the form of a referral fee. You can choose any agent/broker from any company. We simply look for the best person for the job.

Agents are willing to pay the referral fee because we bring you to them. You are how they make a living and you, as an educated consumer, will be prepared for the process, which will save them time and money. It is truly a win-win for everyone.

FOOD FOR THOUGHT

We should all continue learning. The lending market and the real estate market are always changing. Some of these changes are brand new and others are just recycling through as part of the natural cycle the market goes through.

Our Mission

As Smart Moves Consumer Advocates we make life better for real estate consumers and improve the real estate industry by providing education, consulting, and referral services.

We help make our real estate market infertile ground for scammers and other workers of fraud. We increase the number of educated consumers, savvy people, that know how to avoid fraud and other dangers in real estate, making it harder for dishonest people who would take advantage of consumers for their own benefit.

We help improve housing decisions made by consumers, by arming them with the tools they need to evaluate their situation, and look out for their own best interests. We help improve results for consumers and industry professionals by working with consumers to select the best professionals for their specific real estate needs.

We strive to advise consumers as if the decision and direction affected us as our own.

Real Estate Street Smarts

We don't want dishonest people to stay in the business. We want them out. The predator needs prey to survive. If we can all avoid being prey to dishonest people they will have to go away. After all, a man's got to eat!

Do your part by sharing this book with your friends and family. Seek further education to help you on your way. If we all look out for each other we will all go farther and be happier.

Check our website at www.RESmartMoves.com to learn what is new in Real Estate News. **Sign up for our free monthly newsletter.** You will find the real estate related news and market statistics very helpful as you plan your real estate future. Changes are always happening in the world of real estate, and we keep you "in the know".

Real Estate Street Smarts

-Chapter 15-
The Big Pay Off. Make And Implement Your Plan.

There are so many things to consider. It can be overwhelming which is why you eat this elephant one bite at a time. This is where your plan comes in. It is not as important where you are in the process, but that you know where you are going. You will get there; it is just a matter of time.

Successful people start in different situations. There are many examples of poor people who make big money. A good example of this is a young man who grew up on the wrong side of the tracks, so to speak. Elvis Presley was a poor boy who made it as big as big can be. For some he still lives on today.

I am not saying your plan needs to be about money. If you are like me you only want to live on like Elvis for your own family. You have no interest in being so well known, you just want to take great care of your family.

To arrive at any place you desire, you must know where you want to go and what you want when you get there. If you want a new house on a small farm you have a journey ahead of you that starts with preparing to own your first house. Prepare yourself in every way to take your first step toward that expensive farm of your dreams.

It seems like many of us want to start out in a home similar to the home our parents have. We need to remember, it took our parents many years to get where they are, and to get all that they have.

Your first home will not be your dream home, but it is part of the journey to your dream home. Knowing what you need to do to get to your desired destination will help. Then you can work at it one step at a time until you are there.

It is encouraging that in America anyone, no matter who they are, can work to achieve their own personal dream. We choose what we want to do and who we want to be. No one can tell us that our dream is not an option for us.

All dreams require sacrifice. If you want to live your dream you will save money instead of spending all of it. You will work harder. You will make investments to pick up your pace and speed up your arrival time.

When you know where you want to be, and you know where you currently are, you can plan your journey. If your house on a farm will cost one million dollars and you have one home that is worth 200,000 you know that you will need to pay off your home and buy at least four or five more homes as rentals to be paid off. You will pay off your home and buy additional homes (or other investments) as you are prepared to do so. Each step you take brings you closer to your goal.

You will look for ways to increase your investments to bring you closer to your goals. Because you are looking you will find ways to increase your earnings

Consider Real Estate Investments: Real estate investments can be a great part of your investment planning, for most of the same reasons your personal home is a great investment.

For long-term investments rentals provide tax benefits from depreciating the property over 27.5 years as the government allows. Loans are paid down until they are paid off eventually. Any positive cash flow can be used to save money for another rental or to pay off the loan earlier. As home prices go up your equity (wealth or net worth) will go up as well.

Income properties can be "exchanged" without paying taxes on your gain. This is a huge financial advantage and will help you reach your goals faster. You must meet all the conditions of a <u>1031 Exchange</u>, definitely worth looking into. (You can learn about it on our web site.)

Putting twenty percent down, or hopefully more, will make these rentals comfortable and less stressful. At that point they should pay for themselves with the rental income. Some properties are better than others as rentals. Basic, affordable, and generally appealing housing is the best.

Consider what twenty to thirty years of a real estate investment will do for you. When you start out your monthly cash flow may be a break even. Your rent covers your cost but not any extra. In ten to fifteen years your expenses will be close to the same but your rent will likely have increased by fifty to eighty percent.

Remember in my area forty years ago you could rent a home for 125 to 150 dollars a month. Now rents are one thousand to twelve hundred per month. The rents have doubled three times in forty years.

So thirty years down the road your rental that has had a monthly cost of 1,000 to 1,200 will likely rent for about $4,000 per month. After thirty years you will have it paid off so most of the four thousand will be monthly income. That is how you build wealth. Don't refinance the homes, pay them off.

<u>Get better interest rates for your rental</u> by living in it for a few years with owner occupied financing then rent it out.

and your savings. Your desire will drive you to use your means to bring you closer to your goal instead of spending it on other things.

Long-term goals are a culmination of many short-term goals that have been met. You will get there. The only question is when. Half the fun is the adventure of the journey. What fun would it be if someone handed your dream to you? You must know how to earn your dream if you wish to keep it.

Real Estate Street Smarts

Everyone has a different dream. That is the great thing about it. Having one home paid off and enough investments to live on allows incredible freedom and wealth of personal time.

Having money and time to help others will provide more happiness to you than anything you could possibly buy for yourself. Giving is an incredible way of life.

Your time is the most valuable thing you have, and everyone is given the same twenty-four hours in a day. Using some of your time for someone else will give you something you can actually take with you when you die. Your friendships will be one of your true treasures.

Start with the end in mind. Check your progress and direction frequently. Adapt your plan as you go. Be content with the progress you can achieve and enjoy every part of the journey, its value is just as great as the end result.

It won't be as hard as you think it will be. After you learn what it takes and get your momentum going you will travel much faster. When one home is paid off you can take the rent to add to another home to pay it off much faster and so on until they are all paid off. Then you can sell all of them in a 1031 exchange for the farm land you want. You will need to hold the land for a year before moving onto it. It will likely take you a year to build your new home.

You will get there if you don't give up on your dream. The important thing is that you are heading in the right direction. If you are not heading in the right direction, turn around and get moving. Remember all the people who have made it. They did not make it on their first try. It takes many small steps to get to the top. Prepare yourself to be surprised! You may find that your dream ends up being the surprise.

Real Estate Street Smarts

-Glossary-

1031 exchange (page 150) When you trade or exchange a property for another property of equal or greater value and follow the exact steps of selecting and purchasing according to the rules you can delay paying the taxes on the increase. If you never sell you can avoid it period. This is done by always exchanging your real estate investments and not cashing out. Check our website for details and exchange companies. You must set up an exchange before you buy or sell.

10-year interest only mortgage (page 67) This is a variation of the interest only where the loan is interest only for a 10 year period then switches to a full amortized loan over the remaining 20 years. As you can imagine at that point the payment would go up drastically. With this loan the borrower is betting their income will increase in the 10 year period making the home affordable now and in the future. This loan increases risk because we don't know the future.

15- year fixed mortgage (page 66,79) Home loan with a fixed interest rate for the entire 15 year period of the loan. The loan is paid down each month until the balance is zero. These loans have a little lower interest rate because the money is paid back to the bank faster.

2-1 buy down (page 66) Prepaid interest that allows the borrower to have 3 different payment amounts. The first year it is the least expensive with the lowest interest rate then it changes to a new interest rate that is more than the first year and less than the actual and final interest rate and payment that goes from the 3rd year on for the life of the loan. See also buy down.

30-year fixed mortgage (page 65,72-79) Home loan with a fixed interest rate for the entire 30 year period of the loan. The loan is paid down each month until the balance is zero.

3-year ARM (page 67) Mortgage with a fixed rate and payment for 3 years then switches to an Adjustable Rate. Your risk is increased as you may need to keep the loan longer than the 3 year fixed period. The rate is usually a little lower than the 30-year fixed loan to draw people to them.

5-year ARM (page 67) Mortgage with a fixed rate and payment for 5 years then switches to an Adjustable Rate. Your risk is increased as you may need to keep the loan longer than the 5 year fixed period. The rate is usually a little lower than the 30-year fixed loan to draw people to them.

7 year ARM (page 67) Mortgage with a fixed rate and payment for 7 years then switches to an Adjustable Rate. Your risk is increased as you may need to keep the loan longer than the 7 year fixed period. The rate is usually a little lower than the 30-year fixed loan to draw people to them.

ABR designation (page 58) Accredited Buyer Representative. Additional education is required for this designation.

A-frame home (page 94) Home one or two stories tall with a very steep roof that starts low to the ground and ends very high at its roof peak.

Appraisal (page 28,110,130,131) A professional opinion of the value of a property at an exact time. Cannot be for the future. When completed are usually only valid for the person or company that ordered the appraisal and for a limited time (generally 6 months). It's a report with the stated value of the property and information about other properties that are sold or active in the same market and that are comparable to the subject property. This information shows how the Appraiser came up with their professional opinion of value.

Appraisers (page 28,114,139) Professional that provides a report showing their opinion of the value of real estate for a specific property at a specific time.

APR (page 23) Annual Percentage Rate. The total cost of borrowing the money including the closing costs calculated as an annual figure.

ARM (page 67) Adjustable Rate Mortgages. These loans do not have a fixed interest rate. The rate and the payment fluctuate according to the terms of the loan. They are based on a financial index to determine how the rate should change going up or down. The rates are usually lower at first when these loans are made because the lender is not tied into the rate for the life of the loan. If rates go up they go up with it. This loan is risky for the borrower because your cost is not fixed. Only in times with extremely high interest rates would it make it likely that the loan would be adjusting down more than up in the future.

Balloon Payment (page 1,66) A one time payment at a specific date. It usually is the entire balance of the loan remaining. A 15-year balloon payment on a 30-year loan would make it so you only had the loan for 15 years even though your payment is calculated on a 30 year schedule. At the end of 15 years you would still have a large balance due when the balloon payment was needed unless you pay extra.

Buyer's Agent (page 26,59) An agent that represents the buyer in the purchase of real estate.

Buy downs (page 23,66) Prepaid interest paid at closing that buys down the interest rate for a period or all of the loan. This increases the borrowers closing costs but decreases their monthly payments. See also 2-1 buy down.

Buyers market (page 13,17,114) High levels of supply (homes for sale) and low demand (buyers). Real estate prices decline, stay close to the same or raise slowly.

Cabin home (page 95) Homes that are made out of log or homes that are made to look rustic by using log and other natural materials to finish the inside and outside of the home.

Carbon Monoxide (page 98) The exhaust from the gas systems of the home. It is unsafe inside the home and should be properly vented to the outside air. If it is not correct unsafe levels of carbon monoxide can make residents sick or even cause death. Carbon Monoxide detectors should be used to give alarm of unsafe levels inside the home.

CC&R's (page 38,51,110,112,122) Covenants, Conditions, and Restrictions are the rules for the development above and beyond any city or county regulations. These rules recorded on the county records should be followed by all residents (owners and renters) in the development. You can and should check your title for CC&R's prior to buying in the development. CC&R's are not always followed by residents. Enforcement of these rules are done by the HOA. HOA's vary in their level of strict enforcement.

Central Air Conditioning (page 105-106) Air is cooled, moisture is removed from the air and the air is blown into each room in the home.

Closing (page 1,111) Closing happens only after all funds are received and the documents have been recorded changing the ownership of the property.

Closing costs (page 1,9-13,15,23,70,87,130) Money spent for services that are needed to buy or sell a home. Money that goes to lenders, real estate agents, Title companies, Home inspectors, HOA, Appraisers etc. for services rendered.

Comparables (page 33,34,42) homes or land you use to compare your property to. Active, Under Contract, and Sold homes are typically used to make comparisons and calculate value.

Condo (page 38,92) Residential home that has neighbors potentially above, below and to each side of them.

Conforming loans (page 70) Loans that meet the requirements to be sold to Fannie Mae or Freddie Mac. These companies are a partnership of the government and the private sector created by the government to increase money available to potential home owners. These companies buy the loans that are originated by lenders who supply the money in the first place for the loan. This allows them to go lend the same money to another borrower.

Concessions (page 45) Any money or cost for items the seller paid for the buyer, such as, buyer closing cost or HOA transfer fees etc..

Consumer loan amortization chart (page 84) See the actual cost of borrowed money for consumer purchases.

Conventional loan (page 70) Loans not qualified to be insured by FHA and VA. Their requirements are easier to meet and are more cost effective than Jumbo loans because the loan amounts are smaller and less risky for the lender. Their requirements are usually harder than government backed loans. Conventional loans are funded by the private sector as are the rules and availability of the loans.

Co-op (page 92) A stock cooperative is real estate owned by a company for the purpose of controlling who lives there. The residents buy into the company and as a benefit are granted a lease for the property they live in. These companies can decide who they want to approve or not approve.

Credit score (page 68) FICO Scores, Equifax, Transunion, & Experian, calculate a numerical score at a low of 300 up to 850, the best score, based on your credit history and your financial structure (amount and type of debt). These scores are used by lenders to determine what risk you will be for the loan you want. If you do not meet the minimum score requirement for the loan you do not qualify. These scores can also affect other things such as insurance rates you are offered. See also FICO Score.

CRS designation (page 58) Certified Residential Specialist. Additional education is required for this designation.

Culinary water (page 124) Clean water used inside the home. In most cases it is good for drinking water. Water quality can be fixed with systems in place.

Debt to income ratios (page 68) The amount of debt in relation to income calculated as a percentage. Your front end ratio is calculated on the mortgage you are applying for and your back end ratio is calculated on all of your debts to your income. Lenders use these to determine is you are a good candidate for the loan you want. If too much of your income is promised to debt you will not qualify.

Developer (page 18,48,104) Investor that takes raw land, invests money and time to changing zoning and use for the property with the county or city, then installs the utilities, roads, and shapes the land while splitting the large piece of land into smaller pieces of land to be sold to individuals for their use. Raw land is changed to a subdivision.

Down payment (page 9-13,15,70,87) Money the buyer pays toward the purchase of the home, including the earnest money. The balance of the purchase cost is paid for with a home loan secured by the buyer before the closing.

Duplex (page 96) Investment property with two units. Can only be sold as one property.

Early mortgage payoff schedule (page 71) Pay your loan of years earlier by paying a little extra.

Earnest Money (page 87,108,126) Money the buyer puts down at the time they make an offer to a seller to show the seller they are serious. The earnest money is collateral for the contract. The seller will receive the money if the buyer does not meet the terms of the contract. The buyer will receive an equal sum from the seller if the seller does not meet the terms of the contract. When the home closes the money is applied to the buyers down payment as a prepaid deposit.

Escrow (page 52,127) From the day you have an accepted offer to the day the home purchase is finalized and closes including possession of the property changing to the buyer is called escrow. In this time period both buyers and seller work to meet the requirements and perform the tasks stated in the terms of the contract between the two parties.

Evaluations and inspections deadline (page 110,115) Deadline the buyer has to check the property and all aspects of the home purchase to make sure they want to buy the home. After this deadline the buyer may lose their earnest money if they don't buy the home.

Fair Housing (page 124,126) Federal law that you cannot discriminate based on race, color, religion, sex, national origin, familial status or source of income.

FED (page 64,67) Centralized Bank for the United States. They control rates and money supply in the country. The Fed Chairman is one of the most powerful people in the Country. They work to take extreme highs and lows out of the economy by changing the supply and cost of money available for growth.

FHA loans (page 23,65,69,70) Federal Housing Administration. Federally insured loans with special rules guidelines and requirements. Known for requiring less from the borrower than conventional loans.

Flipping (page 141) Buying a home then immediately selling the home.

FICO Score (page 127) A FICO Score is a credit score derived from the credit model developed by Fair Isaac Corporation. It is the best-know credit score in the United States. It considers, payment history, length of credit history, new credit, types of credit used, and debt. See also credit score.

Flood Zone (page 121) Areas designated to have the risk of flood. Risk is measured by years, and how often a flood is expected to happen.

Forced Air heating (page 105) A furnace blows heated air through duct work to each room of the home.

Foreclosure (page 65) The process the bank goes through to take a home from a borrower that does not pay the mortgage.

Good faith estimate (page 23) A bid for the cost of a mortgage loan including program type, interest rate, APR, and payment amounts

Green Belt (page 55) Tax status to keep property taxes low for large pieces of ground that are not developed. They are used for agricultural type uses such as farming and ranching etc..

GRI designation (page 58) Graduate Realtor Institute. Additional education is required for this designation.

High-rise condos (page 97) Condos that are a part of tall multistory buildings with elevators and interior hallways.

HOA (page 5,6,38,51,68,92,96-98,103,110,122) Home Owners Association is the group of owners in a development that are lead by presidents and secretary's from a private company hired by the property owners or by owners themselves that have been elected to be the president or other officer to manage the needs of the development for maintenance, upkeep and enforcing HOA rules. They also supervise any suggestions for improvements to be voted on by the membership. All owners of property who pay into the HOA are members of the association.

Home Inspector (page 29) Professional conducting test and inspections on the condition of the buildings on real estate including all their systems.

Home styles (page 93) Homes come is many styles with different features that affect the look and the use of the home. Many examples are given in chapter 9.

Home warranty plans (page 121) Insurance policy paid for with a one time fee to cover the working items of the home. The warranty company fixes or replaces items covered within the coverage period after you pay a deductible.

Homeowners insurance (page 6,9,68,122) Also referred to as fire insurance or property insurance. It can include other insurance riders such as flood or earthquake for additional cost. Insurance in case you have an accident or disaster. Read the terms carefully to know how much coverage you have and what they do and do not cover. The dollar amount should be enough to replace the home and your belongings if necessary. Lenders also often will require you to pay them in an escrow account that they then use to pay the insurance. Lenders can also put a policy in place if you let your policy lapse and charge you for it. This amount would likely be higher than the cost of a policy if you found one.

Inflation (page 7,63) The value decline of the U.S. dollar increases the cost of all items in dollars. The increased cost is inflation.

Interest only mortgage (page 67) A mortgage that has payments calculated on interest only and no principle. The balance of the loan is NOT paid down at all. The balance is the same at the end of the loan as it is the first day unless extra is paid.

Interest rate (page 1,9,19,20,23,64,65,66) The percentage borrowers pay of the total amount they borrow. Your monthly payment is calculated based on the interest rate you are charged.

Interest tax deduction (page 12) Federal tax deduction home owners can use on the amount of interest they pay on their personal residence. The government could change this tax law. Check with your tax advisor.

Investment rate of return chart (page 84-86) See how much you will make on your invested money.

Investment property (page 70) Any home or land that is purchased without the intent of living in the property. These properties are held for the monetary increase from monthly rent or from the increased total value in the future.

Investor (page 18,63,64,139) An owner of real estate that holds property for the purpose of making money now or in the future.

Irrigation water (page 123) Sometimes called gray water. This water is not treated for drinking and washing inside the home but is used for watering the outside of the property.

Jumbo loans (page 70) High dollar loans that are above the maximum amount required to meet conforming loans. These loans come with higher interest rates because they are more risky. Prices in expensive home fluctuate farther and more often than more affordable housing because of the limited supply of buyers for them.

Keybox or Lockbox (page 57) A secure box that holds the key to your home. Most MLS systems have digital keyboxes that only allow members of the MLS to have access to the keys. They can also have lockout times when the box will not work. Contractor keyboxes use a code similar to a bike lock to open the box. They are used to give access to people that are not part of the MLS system like subcontractors or potential renters etc..

Landlord (page 5,7-9,11) The owner of a home or property that is rented out to the person who lives and uses the property.

Lease agreement (page 5) Written legal contract between a renter and a landlord dictating how much the renter will pay, for how long they have the right to use the property and any rules and restrictions on the use.

Lender letter (page 127) Letter from the buyers lender showing either a pre-approval or an approval for the home loan. An Approval letter is best because the borrower has had their file sent through underwriting and the loan has been approved with a list of condition such as an appraisal and an accepted purchase contract. A pre-approved lender letter states that the borrower should qualify based on what the lender knows about the buyer but the file has not been compiled and sent through for approval yet.

LIBOR index (page 67) London Inter-Bank Offered Rate. An index based on the interest rate five major international banks charge at a given moment. This moves with changes in the financial market.

Limited Agent (page 26) An agent that represents both the buyer and the seller. They are limited as they cannot say anything that will weaken either parties negotiating position.

Listing Agent (page 26,59) An agent that represents the seller in the process of selling real estate.

Long term real estate investments (page 6,8,150) Real estate investments that are kept for ten or more years. Long term investments lower risk. It gives time for the value to increase and the loan, if applicable to be paid down.

Mechanics lien (page 25) Any worker or supplier on real estate has the right to file a lien on the property to help guarantee payment for materials used or labor. Lien is recorded on the county recorders office in the order the lien was recorded. These liens can be wiped out if a prior lien holder like a mortgage forecloses on the property.

Median (page 18,70) The exact middle meaning half of the items compared are higher and the other half are lower. Median price is the price of the home that is exactly in the middle of the homes compared.

Mixed use developments (page 92) Developments with more than one type of real estate such as commercial on the bottom floor and residential units above on the upper levels.

MLS (page 26,42,44,55-57,139) Multiple Listing Service. Database online for the use of agents and then also to the public to search for specific criteria of property that is for sale. The MLS is the most user friendly system available to find the properties that meet a given set of parameters. It contains many searchable field choices so you can be specific as to what you are looking for in a home to help narrow your search down. The MLS also has many tools that are helpful such as maps, mortgage calculators, tax information, market history and statistics.

Mold (page 124) Mold can grow in areas with moisture, wood type materials, and poor ventilation. Some molds are hazardous to the health of certain individuals making them sick.

Mortgage insurance (page 9,68,70) Insurance paid at closing or monthly that provides an insurance policy to the lender in case you default on the loan. The insurance is not required if you put 20% down. The cost of the insurance is lower if you have equity of 10% versus 5%. It is one way lenders help manage their risk. In the event of default the lender would receive a payment from the insurance company to cover some of their losses. After you have paid down your balance to less than 80% you can contact the lender and complete their requirements to have the insurance removed. This will save you money each month.

Mortgage Lenders and Brokers (page 22,63,140) Professionals of many types involved with securing loans for borrowers to refinance their home or buy a new one.

Multilevel home (page 94) Home with 4 or more levels.

Negative Amortization Loans This loan program is only available to select people who personally meet the requirements and also have the equity in their home to qualify. With these loans the borrower lives on the loan by receiving money monthly from the loan. This increases the balance on the loan. Grandparents who need money to get by during their final years are the most likely candidates. It is a way for the parents to take care of themselves by using the equity of their home without having to sell their home to do so. It reduces and could eliminate the proceeds the children would split when the home is sold. I think it is better for parents to eat well and have a good quality of life than to give a higher dollar amount to each child when they die. These loans come with expensive costs that must be evaluated for the situation to see if it is worth it.

Non-Conforming loans (page 70) Loans that do not meet the requirements to be sold to Fannie Mae or Freddie Mac.

Open bid (page 130) With an open bid the seller notifies all interested parties of the highest bid amount to see if anyone is willing to go higher.

One and a half story homes (page 95) Homes that look like ramblers but have an upper level built in the middle of the attic space.

Origination fee (page 1,23) Fee charged by lenders and brokers to help the borrower secure a home loan. Paid at closing. One percent of the loan amount is typical for an origination fee.

Prepayment Penalty (page 71) A penalty or fee if the loan is paid off faster than the terms of the loan. You cannot pay extra each month, refinance, or

Real Estate Street Smarts

pay off the mortgage early. Prepayment penalties will have a term for the penalty. 3 years, 2 years etc.. If you wait until after the term of the penalty period you can then pay extra or pay off the mortgage. It is the way the lender guarantees they will get interest (profit) from you on the loan.

Prime (page 67) Rate set by the FED that determines what the cost will be for banks to borrow money. Some ARM loans are based on the prime rate such as prime + 2 percent to calculate their payment.

Principal Broker (page 25,58) The broker in charge of the other agents and brokers at their real estate office.

Principle (page 31,71-79) The amount you owe on the home. This balance goes down anytime principle payments are made on the loan. Interest only loans do NOT have principle payments.

Property tax recapture (page 55) 5 years of prior tax savings from the time a property is changed from green belt to another use, such as dividing the property into smaller lots. The tax savings is recaptured and must be paid. Some contracts may address who will pay for this cost.

Property taxes (page 6,31,68) Annual taxes based on the value of the property paid to the city or county the property is in to be used for schools or any other government program. This lien on the property comes before any other lien. It is the first item paid when a home is sold in default. It even comes before the first mortgage. This is why lenders often require taxes and insurance to be collected by them from you to be paid by them. That way they know it has been done. They don't want to put their money at risk.

Public sewer system (page 106) Plumbing runs from the home into larger public sewer lines that take the waste to a sewer treatment plant.

PUD (page 37,96) Planned Unit Development. Developments stand out because of noticeable differences in ownership or use of the land. Smaller streets and lots, as an example, can be owned by the development.

Radiant heating or cooling (page 105) Water pipes are run throughout the home that are heated or cooled. These pipes radiate the temperature into the rooms. This system can be zoned for each room or parts of the home.

Rambler (page 93) Home with all above ground living space on one level.

Real Estate Agent (page 26,55,57,58) A licensed sales person.

Real Estate Broker (page 25,58) Agent who has met the education and experience required by the state they are licensed in. They also must pass a state test.

Real Estate Consultant/Advocate (page 27,145-148) Professionals that provide education and consulting to help consumers determine what is best for their own situation.

Real Estate Street Smarts

Real estate cycle (page 8,13,14,18) Fluctuations in supply and demand that affect pricing and other conditions related to housing.

Realtor (page 25,26,58,139) Agents and brokers that are members of the National Association of Realtors. They must pay annual dues to have access to MLS and to be a member. They also must follow the code of conduct.

Rental agreement (page 5) Written legal contract between a renter and a landlord dictating how much the renter will pay, for how long they have the right to use the property and any rules and restrictions on the use.

Rental deposit (page 9,11) Deposit held by Landlord to secure the condition of the property. Damage from a renter is repaired with money from the deposit. The renter may get the deposit back if the property is in the same condition it was in at the beginning of the agreement and the renter does not have a rent balance due.

REO (page 55) Real Estate Owned by a bank. Banks are in the money business and not the real estate business. They sell these REO properties at a discount to sell them quickly and get them off their books and put their money back in use.

Regular mortgage payment schedule (page 71-79) A complete breakdown of how your loan payment works each month for the entire 30 year period.

Secondary Lending Market (page 63) Companies and investors who buy loans and packages of many loans from banks and brokers who originate the loans.

Sellers market (page 13,14,17,18,41,42,114) Low supply of homes for sale and high level of demand with many buyers buying homes. Real estate prices increase moderately to quickly as supply shortages cause buyers to bid up against other buyers competing for the home.

Sellers property condition disclosure (page 51) A disclosure form the seller fills out with what the seller knows about the property and its condition. The seller answers all the questions signs and dates the form and gives the form to the buyer for them to review as part of the buyer's evaluations of the property. The buyer also signs and dates the form showing they received the form and have the information.

Septic system (page 106) The plumbing in the home is run to a tank berried in the yard and then to a leach field to decompose and dispel the waste. If the tank fills the owner must remove the waste or pay a company to do so. Additives are added to help break down the waste.

Settlement deadline (page 111) The deadline to have the loan and other closing document signed by all parties. Funding and recording usually happen a few days after settlement.

Real Estate Street Smarts

Settlement statement (page 71,143) The document you sign at settlement that shows where all the money is going, including all the buyers costs for each item. It is very important to check this document to make sure it is correct with your contract.

Short term real estate investments (page 12) Real estate investment that are 5 years or less. These investments are high risks with the cost to buy of 4 to 10% of the purchase price and the price fluctuation of the market making it possible to have large financial losses. Financial gains on short term investment can happen in a sellers market. Does not include short term flipping.

Silent bid (page 130) The seller does not tell any party the offer price and terms they have received.

Smart house (page 37) Homes that have the systems of the home automated and controlled by a computer.

Sold comparable (page 32) Property that has been sold recently that can be used by appraisers, real estate people, and tax assessors to establish the value of a property by comparison.

Split Entry home (page 94) Home with 2 levels with the entry and front door in the middle of the stairway.

Stable, Balanced or Flat Market (page 8,13,42) Even supply and demand. Home prices stay close to the same.

Staging (page 134) Decorating and preparing the home for sale. Includes everything from cleaning, painting, to furniture choice and placement.

Swamp cooler (page 106) Air conditioning that puts moisture into the air then blows it into the home from a roof mounted system in the center of the home or a window. It does not work well with high humidity.

Title company (page 24,25,122,139) Company that provides closing services, title research, and title insurance.

Title insurance (page 24,25,122) Insurance purchased with a one time fee at closing to protect the insured from Title problems and risks. There is the potential to have serious problems on title costing thousands of dollars. You should always have title work done when you buy real estate.

Title report (page 24,52,112,122) Also called a PR, a report showing the research a title company has done as to what has been recorded on the county records in connection with a specific piece of real estate. It contains many items such as loans on the property, judgments, liens, easements, rights of way, CC&R's, deed restrictions, deed transfer fees, and any rights or claims on the property that have been recorded. The report will also have contact information so you can ask questions regarding the report.

Real Estate Street Smarts

Townhouse (page 92,96) Residential homes with neighbors on either side but not above or below. Can come with garages or small private yards.

Tri-Level home (page 94) 3 level home with half a flight of stairs separating each level.

Twin-home (page 38,91,96) Home that is connected with a common wall to another home. They are not duplexes. Each unit can be owned individually.

Two Story (page 93) Home with two levels above ground.

Uncle Sam (page 48) The United States Government. *We must all be related.*

Under contract (page 40) When an offer is accepted and signed by both parties the home is under contract. It will be under contract until the home is sold or the contract is broken. It should be taken off the market unless stated otherwise in writing.

Utilities (page 105) Energy and systems used to run the home.

VA loan (page 69) Veterans Administration loan. A special loan offered to those who have met the service and other requirements in any of the armed services in the military. You can research these loans at www.homeloans.va.gov These loans have more favorable terms for the borrower as a perk of serving our country.

Water rights (page 124) A right to the use of water from a specific source.

Water shares (page 55,124) Ownership is a share of a water company that provides water to the owners of shares in the area the company serves. Irrigation water amount is divided according to the shares of the owners and the availability of the water.

Yield Spread (page 1,23) The difference between the interest rate the lender/broker offers the borrower and the rate they are quoted by the lender providing the actual money for the loan.